BIRTH
of a
FAN

BIRTH
of a
FAN

EDITED BY
RON FIMRITE

Macmillan Publishing Company
NEW YORK

Maxwell Macmillan Canada
TORONTO

Maxwell Macmillan International

NEW YORK   OXFORD   SINGAPORE   SYDNEY

Macmillan Publishing Company   Maxwell Macmillan Canada, Inc.
866 Third Avenue   1200 Eglinton Avenue East
New York, NY 10022   Suite 200
                                      Don Mills, Ontario M3C 3N1

Macmillan Publishing Company is part of the Maxwell Communication Group of Companies.

Library of Congress Cataloging-in-Publication Data
Birth of a fan/edited by Ron Fimrite.
      p.   cm.
   ISBN 0-02-537760-4
   1. Baseball fans—United States—Biography.   2. Baseball—United States—History.   I. Fimrite, Ron.
   GV863.A1B57   1993   92-16766   CIP
796.357'092'2—dc20
[B]

Macmillan books are available at special discounts for bulk purchases for sales promotions, premiums, fund-raising, or educational use. For details, contact:

                    Special Sales Director
                    Macmillan Publishing Company
                    866 Third Avenue
                    New York, NY 10022

10 9 8 7 6 5 4 3 2 1

Printed in the United States of America

Contents

Introduction

Ostensibly, this is a book about baseball. Actually, it's more about growing up, about learning, about self-exploration. It's my guess that the essayists represented here—this one, certainly—were more than a little surprised to find that, in recounting their baseball beginnings, they found much else to ponder. Baseball, it develops, did not merely transform these writers into terminal fans; it also heightened their awareness of a larger world, introduced them to a life beyond childhood. This is obviously and especially true for those of us who came upon the game in the years before the ubiquitous intrusion of television. Because we craved information, we became, at an early age, avid readers of the newspaper sports pages and the sports magazines, a habit that in time led us to weightier matter in other sections of the paper and finally to books and, yes, writing. Through baseball we as youngsters were introduced to such previously arcane subjects as geography (you had to know where the major league cities were), history (better find out who this guy Dela-

hanty is), and, since ballparks of yesteryear were struc-
tures of considerable individuality and charm, architecture. Even those of us who were abject failures at
mathematics learned how to calculate batting averages
and ERAs. We were involved unknowingly in a primitive
form of scholarship. Lacking the tube as crutch, we were
obliged to work a little harder for news of our heroes then,
and I often—and perhaps presumptuously—think we were
better for the effort. Do kids nowadays learn how to read
because of baseball? With the games on television all the
time, do they read at all?

Baseball also gave at least the male essayists in this
book hyperactive fantasy lives. Mediocre players almost
to a man, the writers were stars in their daydreams,
executing impossible plays with panache, driving home
the winning runs in the World Series, accepting the
plaudits of the press, acclaimed on radio as national
icons. Ah yes, radio. Here, you will read what an important part of our lives that instrument would become. The
women essayists on these pages approach the game with
minds less cluttered by dreams of glory, of course; not for
them the woolgathering of their male counterparts. And
yet, as you will learn, the game also led them to some
important lessons and it held them no less in its thrall.

What we have here, really, is a sort of hot-stove session
among some literary friends of mine, old and new, who
have traveled back into their pasts on a basepath journey
of self-discovery. Along the way, they have found much
to laugh about and even cry over. It is, I'm sure you will
find, a trip well worth taking.

Ron Fimrite
March 1, 1992

BIRTH
of a
FAN

Early Innings

ROGER ANGELL

I was born in 1920, and became an addicted reader at a precocious age. Peeling back the leaves of memory, I discover a peculiar mulch of names. Steerforth, Tuan Jim, Moon Mullins, Colonel Sebastian Moran. Sunny Jim Bottomley, Dazzy Vance, Goose Goslin. Bob La Follette, Carter Glass, Rexford Guy Tugwell. Robert Benchley, A. E. Housman, Erich Maria Remarque. Hack Wilson, Riggs Stephenson. Senator Pat Harrison and Representative Sol Bloom. Pie Traynor and Harry Hopkins. Kenesaw Mountain Landis and Benjamin Cardozo. Pepper Martin. George F. Babbitt. The Scottsboro Boys. Franklin Delano Roosevelt. Babe Ruth. In my early teens, I knew the Detroit Tigers' batting order and FDR's first cabinet, both by heart. Mel Ott's swing, Jimmie Foxx's upper arms, and Senator Borah's eyebrows were clear in my mind's eye. Baseball, which was late in its first golden age, meant a lot to me, but it didn't come first, because I seem to have been a fan of everything at that age—a born pain in the

1

neck. A city kid, I read John Kieran, Walter Lippmann, Richards Vidmer, Heywood Broun, and Dan Daniel just about every day, and what I read stuck. By the time I'd turned twelve, my favorite authors included Conan Doyle, Charles Dickens, Will James on cowboys, Joseph L. Altsheler on Indians, and Dr. Raymond L. Ditmars on reptiles. Another batting order I could have run off for you would have presented some prime species among the Elapidae—a family that includes cobras, coral snakes, kraits, and mambas, and is cousin to the deadly sea snakes of the China Sea.

Back then, baseball and politics were not the strange mix that they would appear to be today, because they were both plainly where the action lay. I grew up in New York and attended Lincoln School of Teacher's College (*old* Lincoln, in Manhattan parlance), a font of progressive education where we were encouraged to follow our interests with avidity; no Lincoln parent was ever known to have said, "Shut up, kid." My own parents were divorced, and I lived with my father, a lawyer of liberal proclivities who voted for Norman Thomas, the Socialist candidate, in the presidential election of 1932 and again in 1936. He started me in baseball. He had grown up in Cleveland in the Nap Lajoie–Addie Joss era, but he was too smart to try to interpose his passion for the Indians on his son's idolatrous attachment to the Yankees and the Giants, any more than he would have allowed himself to smile at the four or five Roosevelt-Garner buttons I kept affixed to my windbreaker (above my knickers) in the weeks before election day in 1932.

The early to mid-1930s were rough times in the United States, but palmy days for a boy-Democrat baseball fan in

New York. Carl Hubbell, gravely bowing twice from the waist before each delivery, was throwing his magical screwball for the Giants, and Joe DiMaggio, arriving from San Francisco in '36 amid vast heraldings, took up his spread-legged stance at the Stadium, and batted .323 and .346 in his first two years in the Bronx. He was the first celebrated rookie to come up to either team after I had attained full baseball awareness: *my* Joe DiMaggio. My other team, the New Deal, also kept winning. Every week in 1933, it seemed, the White House gave birth to another progressive, society-shaking national agency (the AAA, the NRA, the CCC, the TVA), which Congress would enact into law by a huge majority. In my city, Fiorello LaGuardia formed the Fusion Party, routed the forces of Tammany Hall, and, as mayor, cleared slums, wrote a new city charter, and turned up at five-alarmers wearing a fire chief's helmet. (I interviewed the Little Flower for my high-school paper later in the decade, after sitting for seven hours in his waiting room. I can't remember anything he said, but I can still see his feet, under the mayoral swivel chair, not quite touching the floor.) Terrible things were going on in Ethiopia and Spain and Germany, to be sure, but at home almost everything I wanted to happen seemed to come to pass within a few weeks or months—most of all in baseball. The Yankees and the Giants between them captured eight pennants in the thirties, and even played against each other in subway series in 1936 (hello, ambivalence) and again in 1937. The Yankees won both times; indeed, they captured all five of their World Series engagements in the decade, losing only three games in the process. Their 12–1 October won-lost totals against the Giants, Cubs, and Reds in '37, '38, and '39 made me sense at last that winning wasn't everything it was cracked up to be; my later defection to the Red Sox and toward the pain-pleasure principle had begun.

THERE ARE MORE holes than fabric in my earliest baseball recollections. My father began taking me and my four-years-older sister to games at some point in the latter twenties, but no first-ever view of Babe Ruth or of the green barn of the Polo Grounds remains in mind. We must have attended with some regularity, because I'm sure I saw the Babe and Lou Gehrig hit back-to-back home runs on more than one occasion. Mel Ott's stumpy, cow-tail swing is still before me, and so are Gehrig's thick calves and Ruth's debutante ankles. Baseball caps were different back then: smaller and flatter than today's constructions—more like the workmen's caps that one saw on every street. Some of the visiting players—the Cardinals, for instance—wore their caps cheerfully askew or tipped back on their heads, but never the Yankees. Gloves were much smaller, too, and the outfielders left theirs out on the grass, in the shallow parts of the field, when their side came in to bat; I wondered why a batted ball wouldn't strike them on the fly or on the bounce someday, but it never happened. John McGraw, for one, wouldn't have permitted such a thing. He was managing the Giants, with his arms folded across his vest (he wore a suit some days and a uniform on others), and kept his tough, thick chin aimed at the umpires. I would look for him—along with Ott and Bill Terry and Travis Jackson—

the minute we arrived at our seats in the Polo Grounds.

I liked it best when we came into the place from up top, rather than through the gates down at the foot of the lower-right-field stand. You reached the upper-deck turnstiles by walking down a steep, short ramp from the Speedway, the broad avenue that swept down from Coogan's Bluff and along the Harlem River, and once you got inside, the long field within the horseshoe of decked stands seemed to stretch away forever below you, toward the bleachers and the clubhouse pavilion in center. My father made me notice how often Terry, a terrific straight-away slugger, would launch an extra-base hit into that bottomless countryside ("a homer in any other park" was the accompanying refrain), and, sure enough, now and then Terry would reaffirm the parable by hammering still another triple into the pigeoned distance. Everything about the Polo Grounds was special, right down to the looped iron chains that separated each sector of box seats from its neighbor and could burn your bare arm on a summer afternoon if you weren't careful. Far along each outfield wall, a sloping miniroof projected outward, imparting a thin wedge of shadow for the bullpen crews sitting there: they looked like cows sheltering beside a pasture shed in August.

Across the river, the view when you arrived was different but equally delectable: a panorama of svelt infield and steep, filigree-topped inner battlements that was offered and then snatched away as one's straw-seat IRT train rumbled into the elevated station at 161st Street. If the Polo Grounds felt pastoral, Yankee Stadium was Metropole, the big city personified. For some reason, we always walked around it along the right-field side,

never the other way, and each time I would wonder about
the oddly arrayed ticket kiosks (General Admission 55
cents; Reserved Grandstand $1.10) that stood off at such
a distance from the gates. Something about security, I
decided; one of these days, they'll demand to see pass-
ports there. Inside, up the pleasing ramps, I would stop
and bend over, peering through the horizontal slot between the dark, overhanging mezzanine and the descend-
ing sweep of grandstand seats which led one's entranced
eye to the sunlit green of the field and the players on it.
Then I'd look for the Babe. The first Yankee manager I
can remember in residence was Bob Shawkey, which
means 1930. I was nine years old.

I can't seem to put my hand on any one particular game
I went to with my father back then; it's strange. But I
went often, and soon came to know the difference
between intimate afternoon games at the Stadium (play
started at 3:15 P.M.), when a handful of boys and night
workers and layabouts and late-arriving businessmen
(with vests and straw hats) would cluster together in the
stands close to home plate or down in the lower rows of
the bleachers, and sold-out, roaring, seventy-thousand-
plus Sunday doubleheaders against the Tigers or the
Indians or the Senators (the famous rivalry with the
Bosox is missing in memory), when I would eat, cheer,
and groan my way grandly toward the distant horizon of
evening, while the Yankees, most of the time, would win
and then win again. The handsome Wes Ferrell always
started the first Sunday game for the Indians, and proved
a tough nut to crack. But why, I wonder, do I think of Bill
Dickey's ears? In any case, I know I was in the Stadium
on Monday, May 5, 1930, when Lefty Gomez, a twitchy

rookie southpaw, pitched his very first game for the Yankees, and beat Red Faber and the White Sox, 4–1, striking out his first three batters in succession. I talked about the day and the game with Gomez many years later, and he told me that he had looked up in the stands before the first inning and realized that the ticket-holders there easily outnumbered the population of his hometown, Rodeo, California, and perhaps his home county as well.

I attended the Gomez inaugural not with my father but with a pink-cheeked lady named Mrs. Baker, who was— well, she was my governess. Groans and derisive laughter are all very well, but Mrs. Baker (who had a very brief tenure, alas) was a companion any boy would cherish. She had proposed the trip to Yankee Stadium, and she was the one who first noticed a new name out on the mound that afternoon, and made me see how hard the kid was throwing and what he might mean for the Yanks in the future. "Remember the day," she said, and I did. Within another year, I was too old for such baby-sitting but still in need of late-afternoon companionship before my father got home from his Wall Street office (my sister was away at school by now); he solved the matter by hiring a Columbia undergraduate named Tex Goldschmidt, who proved to be such a genius at the job that he soon moved in with us to stay. Tex knew less about big-league ball than Mrs. Baker, but we caught him up in a hurry.

BASEBALL MEMORIES are seductive, tempting us always toward sweetness and undercomplexity. It should not be inferred (I remind myself) that the game was a unique bond between my father and me, or always near the top of my own distracted interests. If forced to rank the preoccupying family passions in my home at that time, I would put reading at the top of the list, closely followed by conversation and opinions, politics, loneliness (my father had not yet remarried, and I missed my mother), friends, jokes, exercises and active sports, animals (see below), theater and the movies, professional and college sports, museums, and a very large Misc. Even before my teens, I thought of myself as a full participant, and my fair-minded old man did not patronize me at the dinner table or elsewhere. He supported my naturalist bent, for instance, which meant that a census taken on any given day at our narrow brownstone on East Ninety-third Street might have included a monkey (a Javanese macaque who was an inveterate biter); three or four snakes (including a five-foot king snake, the Mona Lisa of my collection, that sometimes lived for a day or two at a time behind the books in the library); assorted horned toads, salamanders, and tropical fish; white mice (dinner for the snakes); a wheezy Boston terrier; and two or three cats, with occasional kittens.

Baseball (to get back on track here) had the longest run each year, but other sports got my full attention. September meant Forest Hills, with Tilden and Vines, Don Budge and Fred Perry. Ivy League football still mattered in those times, and I saw Harvard's immortal Barry Wood and Yale's ditto Albie Booth go at each other more than once; we also caught Chick Meehan's NYU Violets, and even some City College games, up at Lewisohn Stadium. Winter brought the thrilling Rangers (Frank Boucher,

Ching Johnson, and the Cook brothers) and the bespangled old Americans: there was wire netting atop the boards, instead of Plexiglas, and Madison Square Garden was blue with cigarette and cigar smoke above the painted ice. I went there on weekends, never on school nights, usually in company with my mother and stepfather, who were red-hot hockey fans. Twice a year, they took me to the six-day bicycle races at the Garden (Reggie McNamara, Alfred Letourner, Franco Georgetti, Torchy Peden), and, in midwinter, to track events there, with Glenn Cunningham and Gene Venzke trying and again failing to break the four-minute mile at the Millrose Games. Looking back, I wonder how I got through school at all. My mother, I should explain, had been a Red Sox fan while growing up in Boston, but her attachment to the game did not revive until the mid-1940s, when she fetched up at Presbyterian Hospital for a minor surgical procedure; a fellow-patient across the hall at Harkness Pavilion was Walker Cooper, the incumbent Giants catcher, drydocked for knee repairs, who kept in touch by listening to the Giants'-game broadcasts every day. My mother turned her radio on, too, and was hooked.

Sports were different in my youth—a series of events to look forward to and then to turn over in memory, rather than a huge, omnipresent industry, with its own economics and politics and crushing public relations. How it felt to be a young baseball fan in the thirties can be appreciated only if I can bring back this lighter and fresher atmosphere. Attending a game meant a lot, to adults as well as to a boy, because it was the only place you could encounter athletes and watch what they did. There was no television, no instant replay, no evening highlights. We saw the players' faces in newspaper photographs, or in the pages of *Baseball,* an engrossing monthly with an invariable red cover, to which I subscribed, and here and there in an advertisement. (I think Lou Gehrig plugged Fleischmann's Yeast, a health remedy said to be good for the complexion.) We never heard athletes' voices or became aware of their "image." Bo Jackson and Joe Montana and Michael Jordan were light-years away. Baseball by radio was a rarity, confined for the most part to the World Series; the three New York teams, in fact, banned radio coverage of their regular-season games between 1934 and 1938, on the theory that daily broadcasts would damage attendance. Following baseball always required a visit to the players' place of business, and, once there, you watched them with attention, undistracted by Diamond Vision or rock music or game promotions. Seeing the players in action on the field, always at a little distance, gave them a heroic tinge. (The only player I can remember encountering on the street, one day on the West Side, was the Babe, in retirement by then, swathed in his familiar camel-hair coat with matching cap.)

We kept up by reading baseball. Four daily newspapers arrived at my house every day—the *Times* and the *Herald Tribune* by breakfast time, and the *Sun* and the *World-Telegram* folded under my father's arm when he got home from the office. The games were played by daylight, and, with all sixteen teams situated inside two time zones, we never went to bed without knowledge of that day's baseball. Line scores were on the front page of the afternoon dailies, scrupulously updated edition by edition, with black squares off to the right indicating latter innings, as yet unplayed, in Wrigley Field or Sportsman's Park. I soon came to know all the bylines— John Drebinger, James P. Dawson, and Roscoe McGowen in the *Times* (John Keiran was the columnist); Rud Rennie and Richards Vidmer in the *Trib;* Dan Daniel, Joe Williams, and Tom Meany in the *World-Telly* (along with Willard Mullin's vigorous sports cartoons); Frank Graham in the *Sun;* and, now and then, Bill Corum, in the *Sunday American,* a paper I sometimes acquired for its terrific comics.

Richards Vidmer, if memory is to be trusted, was my favorite scribe, but before that, back when I was nine or ten years old, what I loved best in the sports pages were box scores and, above all, names. I knew the names of a few dozen friends and teachers at school, of course, and of family members and family friends, but only in baseball could I encounter anyone like Mel Ott. One of the Yankees pitchers was named George Pipgras, and Earle Combs played center. Connie Mack, a skinny gent, managed the Athletics and was in fact Cornelius McGil-icuddy. Jimmie Foxx was his prime slugger. I had a double letter in my name, too, but it didn't match up to a Foxx or an Ott. Or to Joe Stripp. I read on, day after day, and found rafts of names that prickled or sang in one's mind. Eppa Rixey, Goose Goslin, Firpo Marberry, Jack Rothrock, Eldon Auker, Luck Appling, Mule Haas, Adolfo Luque (for years I thought it was pronounced "Lyo-kyoo")—Dickens couldn't have done better. Paul Derringer was exciting: a man named for a pistol! I lingered over Heinie Manush (sort of like sitting on a cereal) and Van Lingle Mungo, the Dodger ace. When I exchanged baseball celebrities with pals at school, we used last names, to show a suave familiarity, but no one ever just said "Mungo," or even "Van Mungo." When he came up in conversation, it was obligatory to roll out the full name, as if it were a royal title, and everyone in the group would join in at the end, in chorus: "Van Lin-gle MUN-go!"

Nicknames and sobriquets came along, too, attaching themselves like pilot fish: Lon Warneke, the Arkansas Hummingbird; Travis (Stonewall) Jackson; Deacon Danny MacFayden (in sportswriterese, he was always *"bespectacled* Deacon Danny MacFayden"); Tony (Poosh 'Em Up) Lazzeri (what he pooshed up, whether fly balls or base runners, I never did learn). And then, once and always, Babe Ruth—the Bambino, the Sultan of Swat.

By every measure, this was a bewitching time for a kid to discover baseball. The rabbit ball had got loose in both leagues in 1930 (I wasn't aware of it)—a season in which Bill Terry batted .401 and the Giants batted .319 as a team. I can't say for sure that I knew about Hack Wilson's astounding 190 RBIs for the Cubs, but Babe Herman's .393 for the Dodgers must have made an impression. (The *lowly* Dodgers. As I should have said before, the Dodgers—or Robins, as they were called in tabloid headlines—were just another team in the National League to me back then; I don't think I set foot in Ebbets Field until the 1941 World Series. But they became the enemy in 1934, when they knocked the Giants out of a pennant in September.) The batters in both leagues were reincd in a bit after 1930, but the game didn't exactly become dull. Lefty Grove had a 31–4 season for the A's in 1931, and Dizzy Dean's 30–7 helped win a pennant for the Gas House Gang Cardinals in 1934. That was Babe Ruth's last summer in the Bronx, but I think I was paying more attention to Gehrig just then, what with his triple-crown .363, forty-nine homers, and 165 runs batted in. I became more aware of other teams as the thirties (and my teens) wore along, and eventually came to think of them as personalities—sixteen different but familiar faces ranged around a large dinner table, as it were. To this day, I still feel a little stir of fear inside me when I think about the Tigers, because of the mighty Detroit teams of 1934 and 1935, which two years running shouldered the Yankees out of a pennant. I hated Charlie Gehringer's pale face and deadly stroke. One day in '34, I read that a Yankee bench player had taunted Gehringer, only to be silenced by Yankee manager Joe McCarthy. "Shut up," Marse Joe said. "He's hitting .360—get him mad and he'll bat .500." Gehringer played second in the same infield with Hank Greenberg, Billy Rogell, and Marv Owen; that summer, the four of them drove in 462 runs.

The World Series got my attention early. I don't think I read about Connie Mack's Ehmke strategem in 1929 (I had just turned nine), but I heard about it somehow. Probably it was my father who explained how the wily Philadelphia skipper had wheeled out the veteran righty as a surprise starter in the opening game against the Cubs, even though Howard Ehmke hadn't pitched an inning of ball since August; he went the distance in a winning 3–1 performance, and struck out thirteen batters along the way. But I was living in the sports pages by 1932, when the mighty Yankees blew away the Cubs in a four-game series, blasting eight home runs. It troubled me in later years that I seemed to have no clear recollection of what came to be that Series' most famous moment, when Babe Ruth did or did not call his home run against Charlie Root in the fifth inning of the third game, out at Wrigley Field. What *I* remembered about that game was that Ruth and Gehrig had each smacked two homers. A recent investigation of the microfilm files of the *Times* seems to have cleared up the mystery, inasmuch as John Drebinger's story for that date makes no mention of the Ruthian feat in its lead, or, indeed, until the thirty-fourth paragraph, when he hints that Ruth did gesture toward the bleachers ("in no mistaken motions the Babe notified the crowd that the nature of his retaliation would be a wallop right out the confines of the park"), after taking some guff from the hometown rooters as he stepped up to the plate, but then Drebinger seems to veer toward the other interpretation, which is that Ruth's gesture was simply to show that he knew the count ("Ruth signalled with his fingers after each pitch to let the spectators know exactly how the situation stood. Then the mightiest blow of all fell"). The *next-* mightiest blow came on the ensuing pitch, by the way: a home run by Lou Gehrig.

I REMEMBER 1933 even better. Tex Goldschmidt and I were in the lower stands behind third base at the Stadium on Saturday, April 29, when the Yankees lost a game to the ominous Senators on a play I have never seen duplicated—lost, as Drebinger put it, "to the utter consternation of a crowd of 36,000." With the Yanks trailing by 6–2 in the ninth, Ruth and then Gehrig singled, and

Sammy Byrd (a pinch runner for the portly Ruth) came home on a single by Dixie Walker. Tony Lazzeri now launched a drive to deep right-center. Gehrig hesitated at second base, but Walker, at first, did not, and when the ball went over Goslin's head the two runners came around third in tandem, separated by a single stride. The relay—Goslin to Joe Cronin to catcher Luke Sewell—arrived at the same instant with the onrushing Gehrig, and Sewell, whirling in the dust, tagged out both runners with one sweeping gesture, each on a different side of the plate. I was aghast—and remembered the wound all summer, as the Senators went on to win the AL pennant, beating out the Yanks by seven games.

Startling things happened in baseball that season. The first All-Star Game was played, out at Comiskey Park, to a full-house audience; Babe Ruth won it with a two-run homer and Lefty Gomez garnered the win. On August 3, Lefty Grove shut out the Yankees, terminating a string (sorry: a skein) of 308 consecutive games, going back almost exactly two years, in which the Bombers had never once been held scoreless. The record stands, unbeaten and unthreatened, to this day. Later that month, Jimmie Foxx batted in nine runs in a single game, a league record at the time; and, later still, Gehrig played in his 1,308th consecutive game, thereby eclipsing the old mark established by a Yankee teammate, Everett Scott, in 1925. *That* story in the *Times*, by James P. Dawson, mentions the new record in a terse, two-graf lead, and brusquely fills in the details down at the bottom of the column, recounting how action was halted after the first inning for a brief ceremony at home plate, when league president Will Harridge presented Gehrig with a silver statuette "suitably inscribed." Then they got back to baseball: "This simple ceremony over, the Yankees went out almost immediately and played like a winning team, but only for a short time." There was no mooning over records in those days.

It's always useful to have two teams to care about, as I had already learned. My other sweethearts, the Giants, moved into first place in their league on June 13 and were never dislodged. On the weekend of the Fourth of July, they gave us something to remember. I was just back from an auto trip to the Century of Progress World's Fair, in Chicago, taken in the company of three schoolmates and a science teacher, all of us crammed into an ancient Packard, and of course I had no ticket for the big doubleheader against the Cardinals at the Polo Grounds. I'm positive I read John Drebinger the next morning, though—and then read him again: "Pitching of a super-man variety that dazzled a crowd of 50,000 and bewildered the Cardinals gave the Giants two throbbing victories at the Polo Grounds yesterday over a stretch of six hours. Carl Hubbell, master lefthander of Bill Terry's amazing hurling corps, blazed the trail by firing away for eighteen scoreless innings to win the opening game from the Cards, 1 to 0. . . . Then the broad-shouldered Roy Parmelee strode to the mound and through semi-darkness and finally a drizzling rain, blanked the St. Louisans in a nine-inning nightcap, 1 to 0. A homer in the fourth inning by Johnny Vergez decided this battle."

Trumpet arias at this glorious level require no footnotes, and I would add only that Tex Carleton, the Cardinal starter in the first game, threw sixteen scoreless innings himself before giving way to a reliever. He was pitching on two days' rest, and Dizzy Dean, the starter and eventual loser of the afterpiece, on one. The first game got its eighteen innings over with in four hours and three minutes, by the way, and the nightcap was done in an hour and twenty-five.

The Giants went the distance in 1933, as I have said, and took the World Series, as well, beating the Senators by four games to one. Hubbell, who had wound up the regular season with an earned-run average of 1.66 (he was voted Most Valuable player in his league), won two games, and Ott drove in the winning runs in the opener with a home run, and wrapped matters up with a tenth-inning shot in the finale. I had pleaded with my father to get us some seats for one of the games at the Polo Grounds, but he didn't come through. I imagine now that he didn't want to spend the money; times were tough just then. I attended the games by a different means—radio. Five different New York stations carried the Series that year, and I'm pretty sure I listened either to Ted Husing, on WABC, or to the old NBC warhorse, Graham McNamee, over at WEAF or WJZ. (Whoever it was, I recall repeated references to the "boy managers"—Bill Terry and the Senators' Joe Cronin, who had each lately taken the helm at the old franchisoo.) I knew how to keep score by this time, and I rushed home from school—for the four weekday games, that is—turned on the big Stromberg-Carlson (with its glowing Bakelite dial), and kept track, inning by inning, on scorecards I drew on one of my father's yellow legal pads. When my father got home, I sat him down and ran through it all, almost pitch by pitch, telling him the baseball.

I WAS PLAYING ball myself all this time—or trying to, despite the handicaps of living in the city and of my modestly muscled physique. But I kept my mitt in top shape with neat's-foot oil, and possessed a couple of Louisville Slugger bats and three or four baseballs, one so heavily wrapped in friction tape that making contact with it with a bat felt like hitting a frying pan. (One of the bats, as I recall, bore lifelong scars as the result of a game of one-'o-cat played with a rock.) Neat's-foot oil was a magical yellow elixir made from cattle bones and skin— and also a password, unknown to girls. "What's a *neat?*" every true American boy must have asked himself at some point or other, imagining some frightful amputation made necessary by the demands of the pastime.

What skills I owned had been coached by my father from an early age. Yes, reader: we threw the old pill around, and although it did not provide me with an instant ticket to the major leagues, as I must have expected at one time, it was endlessly pleasurable. I imagined myself a pitcher, and my old man and I put in long hours of pitch and catch, with a rickety shed (magically known as the Bull Pen) as backstop; this was at a little summer colony on the west bank of the Hudson, where we rented. My father had several gloves of his own, including an antique catcher's mitt that resembled a hatbox or a round dictionary. Wearing this, he would squat down again and again, putting up a target, and then fire the ball back (or fetch it from the weeds somewhere), gravely snapping the ball from behind his ear like Mickey Cochrane. Once in a while, there would be a satisfying pop as the ball hit the pocket, and he would nod silently and then flip the pill back again. His pitching lexicon was from his own boyhood: *inshoot, hook, hard one,* and *drop.* My own drop dropped to earth so often that I hated the pitch and began to shake him off. I kept at it, in season and out, and, when I finally began to get some growth, developed a pleasing roundhouse curve that sometimes sailed over a corner of the plate (or a cap or newspaper), to the amazement of my school friends. Encouraged, I began to work on a screwball, and eventually could throw something that infinitesimally broke the wrong way, although always too high to invite a swing; I began walking around school corridors with my pitching hand turned palm outward, like Carl Hubbell's, but nobody noticed. Working on the screwball one cold March afternoon (I was thirteen, I think), on a covered but windy rooftop playground at Lincoln, I ruined my arm for good. I continued pitching on into high school (mine was a boarding school in northern Connecticut), but I didn't make the big team; by that time, the batters I faced were smarter and did frightful things to my trusty roundhouse. I fanned a batter here and there, but took up smoking and irony in self-defense. A short career.

WHEN I BEGAN writing this brief memoir, I was surprised to find how often its trail circled back to my father. If I continue now with his baseball story, instead of my own, it's because the two are so different yet feel intertwined and continuous. He was born in 1889, and lost his father at the age of eight, in a maritime disaster. He had no brothers, and I think he concluded early on that it was incumbent on him to learn and excel at every sport, all on his own. Such a plan requires courage and energy, and he had both in large supply. A slim, tall, bald, brown-eyed

man, of handsome demeanor (there is some Seneca
Indian blood on his side of the family), he pursued all
sports except golf, and avidly kept at them his whole life.
He was a fierce swimmer, mountain climber, canoeist,
tennis player, fly fisherman, tap dancer, figure skater, and
ballplayer; he was still downhill-skiing in his middle
seventies, when a stern family meeting was required to
pry him from the slopes, for his own good. He was not a
great natural athlete, but his spirit made him a tough
adversary. My Oedipal struggles with him on the tennis
court went on almost into my thirties, but we stayed
cheerful; somewhere along the line, a family doctor took
me aside and said, "Don't try to keep up with him.
Nobody's ever going to do that."

Baseball meant a great deal to my father, and he was
lucky enough to grow up in a time where there were
diamonds and pickup nines in every hamlet in America.
He played first base and pitched, and in his late teens
joined a village team, the Tamworth Tigers, that played
in the White Mountain valleys of New Hampshire,
where he and his mother and sister went on their
vacations. Years later, he told me about the time he and
some of the other Tamworth stars—Ned Johnson, Paul
Twitchell, Lincoln and Dana Steele—formed a team of
their own and took a train up into Canada, where they
played in a regional tournament; he pitched the only
game they got to play, against a much better club
(semipros, he suspected), and got his ears knocked off.
The trip back (he said, still smiling at the pain) was a long
one. Many years after this, on a car trip when he was in
his seventies, my father found himself near the mountains he knew so well and made a swing over to Choc-

orua and Tamworth to check out the scenes of his youth. He found the Remick Bros. General Store still in business, and when he went in, the man at the counter, behind the postcards and the little birchbark canoes, was Wadsworth Remick, who had played with him on the Tigers long ago. Waddy Remick. There were no signs of recognition, however, and my old man, perhaps uncomfortable in the role of visiting big-city slicker, didn't press the matter. He bought a pack of gum or something, and was just going out the door when he heard, "Played any first base lately, Ernest?"

I think people gave up with reluctance in olden days. My father sailed through Harvard in three years, making Phi Beta Kappa, but he didn't make the varsity in baseball, and had to settle for playing on a class team. Most men would call it a day after that, but not my father. He went to law school, got married, went off to the war in France, came back and moved from Cleveland to New York and joined a law firm—and played ball. I think my very first recollection of him—I was a small child—is of standing beside him in a little downstairs bathroom of our summer place while he washed dirt off his face and arms after a ball game. Rivers of brown earth ran into the sink. Later that same summer, I was with my mother on the sidelines when my father, pitching for some Rockland County nine, conked a batter on the top of his head with an errant fastball. The man fell over backward and lay still for a moment or two, and my mother said, "Oh, God—he's done it!" The batter recovered, he and my father shook hands, and the game went on, but the moment, like its predecessor, stayed with me. Jung would envy such tableaux.

Years passed. In the summer of 1937, I worked on a small combined ranch and farm in northern Missouri, owned by a relative who was raising purebred white-faced Herefords. I drove cattle to their water holes on horseback, cleaned chicken coops, and shot marauding evening jackrabbits in the vegetable garden. It was a drought year, and the temperature would go well over a hundred degrees every afternoon; white dust lay on the trees. I was sixteen. Both the Giants and the Yankees were steaming toward another pennant in New York (it was the DiMaggio, Henrich, Rolfe, Crosetti Yankees by now), but I had a hard time finding news of them in the austere, photoless columns of the Kansas City *Star*. All I could pick up on the radio was Franc Laux doing Cardinals games over KMOX.

My father arrived for a visit, and soon discovered that there would be a local ball game the next Sunday, with some of the hands on the ranch representing our nearby town. Somehow, he cajoled his way onto the team (he was close to fifty but looked much younger); he played first base, and got a single in a losing cause. Late in the game, I was sent up to pinch-hit for somebody. The pitcher, a large and unpleasant-looking young man, must have felt distaste at the sight of a scared sixteen-year-old dude standing in, because he dismissed me with two fiery fastballs and then a curve that I waved at without hope, without a chance. I sat down again. My father said nothing at the time, but later on in the day, perhaps riding back to supper, he murmured, "What'd he throw you—two hard ones and a hook?" I nodded, my ears burning. There was a pause, and Father said, "The curveball away can be very tough." It was late afternoon, but the view from my side of the car suddenly grew brighter.

It is hard to hear stories like this now without an accompanying inner smirk. We are wary of sentiment and obsessive knowing, and we feel obliged to put a spin of psychology or economic determinism or bored contempt on all clear-color memories. I suppose someone could say that my father was a privileged Wasp, who was able to pursue some adolescent, rustic yearnings far too late in life. But that would miss the point. My father was knowing, too; he was a New York sophisticate who spurned cynicism. He had only limited financial success as a Wall Street lawyer, but that work allowed him to put in great amounts of time with the American Civil Liberties Union, which he served as a long-term chairman of its national board. Most of his life, I heard him talk about the latest issues or cases involving censorship, Jim Crow laws, voting rights, freedom of speech, racial and sexual discrimination, and threats to the Constitution; these struggles continue to this day, God knows, but the difference back then was that men and women like my father always sounded as if such battles would be won in the end. The news was always harsh, and fresh threats to freedom immediate, but every problem was capable of solution somewhere down the line. We don't hold such ideas anymore—about our freedoms or about anything else. My father looked on baseball the same way; he would never be a big-league player, or even a college player, but whenever he found a game he jumped at the chance to play and to win.

If this sounds like a romantic or foolish impulse to us today, it is because most of American life, including baseball, no longer feels feasible. We know everything about the game now, thanks to instant replay and computerized stats, and what we seem to have concluded is that almost none of us are good enough to play it. Thanks to television and sports journalism, we also know everything about the skills and financial worth and private lives of the enormous young men we have hired to play baseball for us, but we don't seem to know how to keep their salaries or their personalities within human proportions. We don't like them as much as we once did, and we don't like ourselves as much, either. Baseball becomes feasible from time to time, not much more, and we fans must make prodigious efforts to rearrange our profoundly ironic contemporary psyches in order to allow its old pleasures to reach us. My father wasn't naïve; he was lucky.

ONE MORE THING. American men don't think about baseball as much as they used to, but such thoughts once went deep. In my middle thirties, I still followed the Yankees and the Giants in the standings, but my own playing days were long forgotten; I had not yet tried writing about the sport. I was living in the suburbs, and one night I had a vivid dream, in which I arose from my bed (it was almost a movie dream), went downstairs, and walked outdoors in the dark. I continued down our little patch of lawn and crossed the tiny bridge at the foot of our property, and there, within a tangle of underbrush, discovered a single gravestone. I leaned forward (I absolutely guarantee all this) and found my own name inscribed there and, below it, the dates of my birth and of the present year, the dream time: "1920–1955." The dream scared me, needless to say, but providentially I was making periodic visits to a shrink at the time. I took the dream to our next session like a trophy but, having recounted it, had no idea what it might mean.

"What does it suggest to you?" the goodly man said, in predictable fashion.

"It's sort of like those monuments out by the flagpole in deep center field at the Stadium," I said. Then I stopped and cried, "Oh . . . *Oh*," because of course it had suddenly come clear. My dreams of becoming a major league ballplayer had died at last.

Baseball in My Blood

ROY BLOUNT, JR.

I wonder whether I might have lived a more purposeful life if I had played some position other than outfield in my first years of organized baseball, in 1952 and '53, when I was ten and eleven.

Great demands were not made on Little League outfielders in my time. The best players were pitchers, shortstops, and, to some extent, catchers and first basemen. Our park lacked fences, and we outfielders were expected mainly to keep the long ball from going to ridiculous lengths. Nothing throws off the tempo of a game more than a winded and perhaps even tearful outfielder still scrambling, long after the bases have cleared, to retrieve the horsehide from a crowd of slightly smaller children under a jungle gym, as he half-hears distant cries from the game he had been involved in: "Use another ball. Let's go on without him."

So basically you tried to keep the ball in front of you, and if you didn't you regarded it as gone. I took part in the second Little League game ever played in Decatur, Georgia, and I caught one fly ball in two years in the outfield. For a while I filled my time in the field by chattering to the pitcher: "Come baby come boy you the baby you the boy, humbabyhumboy."

My chatter reached its apogee when Tom Hay was pitching. I would shout, "HeyTomHayheybabyTomTom, hey, Hay. HumbabyTombabyTomHaybabybabyhumTom-TomHayhumTomTom, you the baby, you the one. Fir't by'im baby, heyTomHay, hey baby, heyTomTomTom-TomHayBabyheybabyboy. Hey, TomTomHay, hey," until our coach called me in from left to suggest that my chatter was one of the main reasons Tom had hit so many batsmen that inning.

After that I had a lot of idle time on defense, and I began to muse. I'm musing now. I believe I could tell you how reading, eating, arguing, drollery, and other enthusiasms became ingrained in my fiber, but baseball I don't know.

Since *Field of Dreams*, people assume of every male American that (a) what is wrong with him and (b) why he cares so much about baseball is that his father played catch with him and then made him figure out everything else himself.

But my father did not invest much emotion in baseball. I don't recall ever playing catch with him, or following a pennant race with him. He was a business executive and a Depression survivor who didn't have much time for sports when he was a boy because he worked several part-time jobs to help support his younger siblings. When I was a boy his recreations were catching fish to fry and doing needful carpentry in the home. In one of my strongest visual recollections of him, he is awash in sweat, gritty with dust, and almost violently absorbed in ripping out plaster and lath to expand the kitchen, and my mother is nagging him to take me down to the local swimming pool to teach me to swim. He is reluctant to tear himself away from his handiwork, but he does, and I have a vague memory of thrashing towards him over gradually increasing distances (*very* gradually increasing, and he seems distracted) of chlorinated water. His father—a carpenter and small contractor who talked him out of his true calling, construction, because of the Depression—had taught him to swim by throwing him out of a rowboat.

My father was passably familiar with sports, and he must have played some ball, because I remember running around at a very early age with his old, cracked, hardly-any-webbing glove. And I remember dancing around the house in anticipation of his taking me to see the Atlanta Crackers (Southern Association, Double A) in old Ponce de Leon park. I had read somewhere that in America, the land of the free, I had the right to throw a pop bottle at the umpire, and I was disappointed when my father told me I couldn't.

However, I liked the bleachers, which is probably where I first heard raffish talk: rank, beery guys betting on every pitch and yelling at the umpires. (If these guys weren't throwing things, I had to admit that my father must be right.) Also yelling at the players. Not only at the visitors, who might have been the Memphis Chicks or the Birmingham Barons (for whom Charlie Finley was once a batboy, and who are now owned by the Japanese) or the Mobile Bears or the Nashville Vols or the Chattanooga Lookouts or the New Orleans Pelicans or the Little Rock Travelers (also called the Pebs, short for Pebbles), but also at Crackers who popped up or booted plays. These guys in the bleachers seemed to feel more on top of things than the players. I didn't quite approve of this presumption, but it was striking; when I got into sportswriting, the press box was like that.

After the game you could run down onto the field and ask for autographs; I remember doing this once and being flatly ignored by Dixie Walker, the manager. The Crackers had several old Dodgers who were playing out the string after their big-league careers: Whitlow Wyatt, Hugh Casey, Kirby Higbe. Crackers who went on to the majors included future Hall-of-Famer Eddie Mathews (who hit a ball all the way over the magnolia tree on the bank in deepest center field), Art Fowler, Leo Cristante, Chuck Tanner, and Dick Donovan, a power-hitting pitcher who once hit a 117-mile home run: it cleared the right-field billboards and landed in a freight train going to Chattanooga.

In my first year covering baseball for *Sports Illustrated* I saw Eddie Mathews in a coffee shop. I started to go over and tell him that I had been a big fan of his since he was eighteen and I was eight, but then he ordered coffee in a voice that sounded like a backhoe scooping riprap. To this day I have never heard morning-after so forcefully expressed.

As a boy I planned to bridge the gap between me and the players by growing up to become one, in fact an immortal. Through two years of indifferent Little League outfielding I waited to develop, and when I was twelve I became an all-star third baseman. I played ground balls off my chest, like Pepper Martin (and I knew about Pepper Martin, too, because I was a reader), and hit .320, very close to DiMaggio's lifetime average; I was on course. My father never discussed my baseball career plans with me except once when he suggested I might want to become a sports*writer*. I chuckled inwardly.

The first person I distinctly remember playing catch with is myself. And this may be how my personality started to get scattered, because neither of us was me. I was in the side yard bouncing a tennis ball off the side of the house, being a pitcher throwing at the corners of a bush that defined the strike zone up against our house's stone foundation, and then I was the fielder scooping up the ground ball, and then I was the first baseman digging out the throw. Or I would deliver a fastball that was a little too sweet in the bush there, so I'd move in and throw the ball up against the wooden part of the house at such an angle that it drove me back, back, all the way to the drainage ditch, where I would make an incredible leaping catch.

But by that time I had been seriously involved in baseball, in my own mind, for several years. When did I break in?

Football was the biggest sport around, because Georgia Tech and Georgia were national powers, but all the boys I knew liked baseball. We played games in my side yard, with all the bases but no right field (that's where the woods were), no left field (that's where the house was, but there was a good deal of left-center beyond it), and no catcher (therefore no stealing). Third base was a big square can in which my father carried out clinkers from the furnace until we converted from coal to natural gas, and in which I would sometimes keep a captured box turtle for several days (with lettuce). Clinkers were nasty spiked chunks of uncombustible coal-impurity residue. Traces of clinker cropped up in the yard, so we didn't slide much.

We also played flies and grounders: one player threw the ball up and hit it until one of the others caught three flies and six grounders and got to take a turn batting. Or roll-a-bat: one player threw the ball up and hit it and then laid the bat down in front of the plate, and the fielders tried to throw the ball so as to hit the bat and take it over.

But I was the only one who read baseball history. My father brought me, from one of his business trips, a book called *Big-Time Baseball,* in which I learned about the greatest players of all time, and the great moments (Cookie Lavagetto breaking up Floyd Bevens's Series no-hitter, Mickey Owen dropping the third strike, *the day after I was born*), and the screwballs—I can remember a picture of Rube Waddell from that book more clearly than I can remember the faces of the boys I played with. I don't think any of my friends had done enough baseball scholarship to know about the Hall of Fame, which I planned to be a member of, and I don't think any of them played baseball solitaire the way I did. One day I was absorbed in throwing the ball up and hitting it to certain spots so as to create an imaginary game, when I heard someone say, "Is that as far as you can hit it?"

I looked up and it was Mr. Elliott, our neighbor from across the street, the semipro softball pitcher. His daughter Jerry Lynn was a friend of mine, and sometimes we would go to his games, in which he struck nearly everybody out. He threw a rise ball that I can still see; it would seem to upshift in midair, like Michael Jordan. That day Mr. Elliott came over, I'll bet he was wanting to show a boy some stuff. His son, Neil, was still just a little kid. But I didn't have sense enough to be responsive; my horizons were too unreal. I muttered something and Sambo Elliott went back home. Years later I attended a ceremony honoring him as one of the first members of the Softball Hall of Fame.

I would also make up box scores featuring my name and several imagined or borrowed ones. I remember once when my friend Francis Rowe happened to see one of those box scores, with Blount batting third and Rowe fourth. I think Blount was four-for-five that day (the hardest thing was keeping Blount's batting average within the bounds of credibility) and Rowe got only a couple of hits. Francis gave me a funny look, whether because of the disparity in hits or because of finding himself statistically fictionalized. "You hit more home runs than I do," I said lamely. By that time I was far gone into what I might call—if that movie didn't strike me as so soppy—the field of dreams.

One summer I visited relatives in Baltimore, and shocked my cousin and his friends by consistently hitting balls completely out of his row-house backyard. It was the only time I've ever been regarded as a slugger. I was just used to a bigger playing field.

My mother, the font of family stories, never told any about infant me and baseball. Infant me and nearly everything else. Infant me and my father, for instance. One of her favorites was about the time my father consented to take the middle-of-the-night feeding, and she heard me bellowing and got up and found my father asleep with the bottle in one hand and me, just out of its reach, in the other arm. Apparently I had a great zest for driving nails in boards ("Hammer-nail, Daddy, hammer-nail," my mother used to quote me as exclaiming), but that waned before I can remember.

I mean I like to drive a nail, but I don't put myself to sleep at night driving nails in my head, I put myself to sleep at night hitting line drives in my head. Or pitching. Maybe if my father had encouraged my nailing early on, I would be more firmly rooted today in the physical world, but you never know.

I'll tell you what I remember doing a great deal of, when I was a child: looking for balls I had hit, in my reverie, into the woods beyond center field. Poking around under old leaves, looking for an old ball that was tan and scuffed or even covered with friction tape instead of horsehide; sometimes turning up a moldy brick-hard relic lost many rains before. A mildewed ball is an awful thing, of course, but there's something to be said for the feel of a soft scuffed one, and even one of those black taped-up jobs had a certain charm to its tactility, until the tape began to unwind and get dirty on the sticky side so that you had to keep interrupting play to cut off a bit of the tape, and the ball got smaller and smaller. The game itself is complex enough, without the ball becoming a problem.

Memories are a lot like dreams, but I think it's true that one day during recess on the playground (in the, I don't know, second grade?), we were playing football, and somebody mentioned baseball, and I said, "I hate baseball," and then it dawned on me that I didn't.

Not much of an anecdote, but it seems significant that

I remember very few snatches of conversation from grade school and that is one of them.

I'm sitting here now thinking back, trying to think what other fragments I remember from the first few years of grade school and whether I actually do remember that one. Because another, curiously parallel, fragment has floated up, and I'm sure that I do remember that one, because I'd rather not.

I'm standing in the same spot where I remember saying I didn't like baseball. I'm telling Jody, a pretty girl in my class (I think this may actually be first grade), that I hate Maylene (we will call her), and to my surprise Jody is not siding with me but coming on the great liberal— demanding to know *why* I hate Maylene. It hits me that I hate Maylene because she is dumb, rednecky, and bad-looking; and what kind of person does that make me? Still today, I remember a resentful look on poor old Maylene's boney-nosed face (maybe she was *listening* to my conversation with Jody) that makes me wince. So maybe I have transformed the memory of saying I hated Maylene, and then realizing I shouldn't, into a memory of saying I hated baseball and then realizing I loved it. I was an American boy. Maybe I had a mean streak (to be fair, Maylene was not sweet-tempered), but I had love in my heart for *baseball.*

Here's a moment I remember from my earliest playing days, second grade I guess. I'm just learning the game. My position is what we called "hindcatcher." (In his autobiography Jimmy Carter says that when he was growing up in Georgia they used that term to refer to a boy who stood behind the catcher in case of passed balls, but it was our term for catcher.) With a big run on base I allow a pitch to get away from me—a long, long way away from me—and I'm forever trying to get a handle on it and the guy comes all the way around to score, and my teammates yell at me. My friend David Leveritt (who later died piloting an Air Force jet) runs up to me and says, "I know what you were doing. You were trying to pull that trick in the story."

We had read a story in class about an unpopular boy who won his fellows over to him by letting a ball get past him, luring the runner off base and then throwing him out.

"Yeah," I say.

Lying.

Don't I remember anything favorable about myself in baseball? Well, in one game when I was twelve I made so many sparkling plays—in spite of a jammed thumb on my throwing hand—that Bobby Garner, who was pitching, took me over to the refreshment stand and bought me an Orange Crush. That was a good drink.

Once our coach was advising us (erroneously, we now know) to take salt tablets and avoid drinking much water while playing in the sun so we wouldn't pass out. He distributed tablets but ran out when he came to me. He looked at me as if I were solid and said, in a nice way, "Blount doesn't need salt, he's too dumb to faint." Prone already to overintellectualization (at least by community standards), I was greatly heartened by this compliment. Still am. I never pass out. Or vomit, either. And when I cut my hand outdoors I just keep on working, dirt and blood mixing together. I admired the old Baltimore Orioles, who (I read somewhere) would just rub a split finger in the dirt, or spit tobacco juice on it, and play on.

(Of course if you look at the record books you'll notice
that those old guys in fact tended to miss twenty, thirty,
forty games a year.)

I hustled. I ran things out and slid hard and got my
uniform dirty and held the ball down in front of the base
so the runner had to slide into it and I stayed down on the
ball to dig those short hops out. I liked to have a layer of
clay-dust and the odd blade of grass stuck to me by sweat.

I say that, but now that I think about it, I probably
should have been drinking more water, because I recall
getting sluggish on ninety-five-degree afternoons, which
were common. I berated myself for it, though.

I thought too much. They tell you to "stay within
yourself" in sports, just do what you're capable of, but
that was too depressing a prospect for me. Once, before a
game, Johnny Tingle, our second baseman, and I were
reflecting about not having turned a double play all
season, and I took the position that a *triple* play ought to
be pretty easy to pull off. You'd just have to have two
slow runners on base and nobody out and a sharp ground
ball hit over third. . . .

Which is exactly what occurred in the first inning. A
sign. To me. From the baseball gods. As I moved to my
right toward the perfectly playable ball I saw the whole
thing in my mind: I'd snag that big hop I saw coming and
plant my foot on third and whirl and throw to good old
Tingle (he later married LaMerle Thompson, who thus
became LaMerle Tingle, which undoubtedly was a factor
in her being singled out by a *New York Times* reporter, in
the sixties, for a spirited quote about the effect on her of
Elvis in concert), and with a light of recognition in his
eyes he'd take my chest-high throw and pivot, and over

to first—a triple play! I'm on my way, now. What a story this will make, when I'm interviewed at the height of my fame: in Little League, I started a triple play! A predestined triple play!

I completely missed the big hop.

At least I was integrated enough to grasp the historic opportunity to root for Jackie Robinson. I don't recall being offended as a boy by the fact that the Crackers' home right-field seats were called, with unconscious grinding irony, "the nigger bleachers," but Robinson and Bob Feller were my first favorite big-league players. (My favorite Crackers aside from Eddie Mathews were Ebba St. Claire, Junior Wooten, Bob Montag, and Ralph "Country" Brown.)

I still have a Jackie Robinson comic book, preserved in *My Book of Baseball (and Other Sports)*, a scrapbook I began keeping. . . .

Well, it's hard to say when I began keeping it. One clipping—which says Robin Roberts is in the spring of his sophomore year—would seem to be from the spring of '49, and there's a comic-book page promoting Tootsie Rolls and *The Babe Ruth Story* which, according to the reference books, came out in '48. So I guess I was enough of a baseball fan to be tearing things out about it when I was not yet *eight*. But most of the things in the book that can be dated are from '50 and '51.

The only clipping with a full date on it is an interesting item: the "Big League Averages" from May 27, 1951. Oh. What I thought was particularly interesting about it was that a pitcher was the leading hitter in both leagues: Mel Parnell at .412 (seven-for-seventeen) and Hal Jeffcoat at .500 (one-for-two). But on checking the *Baseball Ency-*

clopedia I see that Jeffcoat wasn't a pitcher then, he was an outfielder. Anyway, Mickey McDermott was sixth in the American at .357 and Ewell Blackwell was sixth in the National at .400. Strange that the papers would allow pitchers' batting averages to take up so much space. Also listed among the top twenty NL hitters were Robin Roberts, Murry Dickson, Jim Konstanty, and a Pirate pitcher I don't remember, Bill Werle. The real leaders in the batting-crown race that May were Jackie Robinson, who was rattling along at .415, and Ferris Fain, .383.

Let's see. Robinson eventually slipped down to third that year, behind Stan Musial and Richie Ashburn, but Fain went on to win the AL's silver bat. I am drifting off into the *Baseball Encyclopedia* , now. (Did you know that there was a Chicken Wolf—legal name William Van Winkle Wolf—who played, in the 1880s and '90s, every position at one time or another; and a Chicken Hawks who played first base and the outfield in the '20s? Throw in Chicken Stanley, Pete LaCock, and Doug "the Red Rooster" Rader and you've got the nucleus of an all-chicken team, even without Chick Stahl and Chick Gandil. And, by the way, Mickey McDermott had 619 at-bats in his career, about a season's worth, and averaged .252 with nine home runs, twenty-nine doubles, seventy-one runs, and seventy-four RBIs—not half bad. And fifty-two walks. One year he had a slugging percentage of .510, and he got a hit in his only World Series at-bat.)

I dare say there is some deep psychological truth at the bottom of my baseball memories, which is not to be found in the *Baseball Encyclopedia. I'm* not even to be found in the *Baseball Encyclopedia.* The only thing that used to worry me about my eventual appearance in the

Baseball Encyclopedia was that my birthplace would be given as Indianapolis because my parents happened to live there briefly, and I wanted to be included whenever people started talking about the best players born in Georgia: Ty Cobb, Johnny Mize, Cecil Travis, Bill Terry, Nap Rucker, Dixie Walker (but not Harry), the regrettably obscure Ivy Wingo, Spud Chandler, Jackie Robinson.

What I started to say is that my scrapbook preserves a Fawcett *Jackie Robinson* comic book from 1950. "There was just one way to answer the taunts and Jackie found it by singling to right!" Old photographs of my family, even of my dogs, are mysterious to me, but every panel in that Jackie Robinson comic book jumps out at me like a lifelong friend. Lots of great stuff about epic struggles between the Dodgers and the Cardinals. The anonymous artist had a great way of capturing a hitter swinging and connecting in one more-lasting-than-video image, with comments popping in from all sides.

"WHAM!"

"ATTA BOY, STAN!"

"MUSIAL AND SLAUGHTER! YEOW!"

The first pennant race I remember was the 1950 one: the Phillie Whiz Kids, Curt Simmons and Robin Roberts and Puddin' Head Jones and Richie Ashburn and Granny Hamner, and Jim Konstanty pitching in an unheard-of seventy-four games. But I was rooting for the Dodgers because of Jackie.

Though I have to admit that in '51 I switched over to the Giants and Willie Mays. You could hardly help it, if you had no geographical affiliation. The Miracle Giants came from thirteen and a half games behind in August to tie the Dodgers at the end of the regular season. Mays and

Monte Irvin and Jim Hearn (from Georgia) and Whitey Lockman and Eddie Stanky. I ran home from school to watch the final innings of the final playoff game (*the day before my tenth birthday*), got there in time to see Bobby Thomson win it with his epochal three-run homer. I was dancing around gleefully and couldn't understand why Georgia Stockton, who came to our house once a week to iron and clean, couldn't share my enthusiasm. She did have an affiliation, with the Dodgers. Twenty-some years later I thought of her when Dick Allen told me he grew up in Wampum, Pennsylvania, rooting for the Dodgers: black people everywhere were Dodger fans then, he said, because of Jackie Robinson.

When I was thirteen we moved to Dallas for half a year, and my father's colorful business associate W. O. Bankston, the Packard dealer, took me and my friend Eddie Guepe (if Eddie should by any chance read this, what became of you?) to the home of Dizzy Dean. Ol' Diz was himself all over, tried to give me a ball autographed by the Gashouse Gang but his wife wouldn't let him. He said his brother Paul's son might make a pitcher; ever since the boy was a baby he and Paul had pulled on his fingers a lot, because long fingers were vital in pitching.

Bankston also took me around to the Dallas police station. In the same halls where Jack Ruby later shot Lee Harvey Oswald, I heard a lawyer tell Bankston, "I had my witness all set to say what I wanted him to and then the son of a bitch got up there and told the *truth*," and I was shocked. But also pleased. My father was too upstanding to bring me into contact with revelations like that.

Maury Wills told me that he got interested in baseball, around the same time I did, when he heard about Jackie

Robinson breaking the color line for the Dodgers in Brooklyn, New York. Until that moment, growing up in Washington, D.C., he'd never heard of the Dodgers, Brooklyn, New York, or baseball. But he decided he wanted to be a baseball player himself.

After he had become one—captain of the Dodgers, in fact—a reporter came to get Wills's reaction to something Robinson had said: that the trouble with the post-Robinson Dodgers was they had no leaders. Wills's reaction was, "What the fuck does Jackie Robinson know?" When that got back to Robinson, he wrote Wills a letter chiding him for letting a reporter provoke him into saying such a thing. Not long thereafter, Robinson died. One of Wills's great baseball regrets is he never answered his inspiration's letter.

I guess I'll never figure out exactly what inspired me to love baseball so much. But if my father were still alive, *maybe* I would be uninhibited enough to share with him this theory:

The sweat and dirt of baseball evoke for me my father working on the house. And the reason I have felt so good when I hit a line drive—or even just saw and heard a line drive hit—is because, hey: good wood. (My father loved wood.) And something hard but responsive hit square, the way my father drove a nail.

("When you take over a pitch and *line* it somewhere," Reggie Jackson told me once, "it's like you've thought of something and put it with beautiful clarity. Everyone is helpless and in awe. Included in your ability are your philosophies, your theories. You tap that mental reservoir and it *goes.*")

And here's something I've been wanting to say since I

was fifteen and my Babe Ruth League team had a father-son game. My father was less than deft at third base but he hit a clean line single, to left, off our best pitcher, Doodle Crane. Doodle used to lie back with his girlfriend next to the bench between innings and *rub her bare leg*, but that's another story. What I want to say is,

CRACK!

ATTA BOY, DADDY!

YOU THE BABY, YOU THE BOY!

Hating Doris

MARY CANTWELL

In truth, I am not a fan. I don't know the names of the players and I am confused about what city has what franchise, and the leagues have been split into divisions that I choose not to recognize. Recently, I read something about a possible Japanese purchase of some share of some team. "The gall!" some people said, but I could summon no more than a yawn. The game will stay a game, won't it? It will still be nine men trying to outhit and outcatch nine other men, and afternoon shadows darkening the playing field until the floods come on and make the paling sky look sick.

My colleagues are mostly males, and on opening day a few of them don't show up at the office. Later they say they had to go to their grandmother's funeral, and then there are great bursts of laughter and an all-round jabbing of elbows. But I distrust the ho-ho-hos and the nudges to the ribs. I think they are simply observing a ritual, honoring an old custom. Showing up for the season's first

pitch is one of the ways they know they are men. A real
fan, I figure, is a fan for all innings. A real fan doesn't wait
for the World Series, as my colleagues do, to start
ho-ho-hoing again.

Once in a while, though, around the end of August,
when I am flipping through the sports pages on my way
to the crossword, a headline catches my eye. The Red Sox
are in second place. Or third place. Or maybe even in
first. Then I feel as I do when the drums roll and the
high-school kids lift their cornets at the start of my
hometown's Fourth of July parade. My stomach flutters,
my eyes get damp around the edges, and my ribs get tight
around my heart. "Maybe this time," I say to myself,
knowing all the time that I know better.

Now I can scarcely believe it, the way it was for me on
the hot summer mornings when we—my parents, a
friend of theirs, and my sister, the Yankees fan—headed
north on Route 1. Past Pawtucket, shabbiest of mill
towns, we went, and Narragansett Race Track, and the
two Attleboros, and the shallow ponds and skinny trees
that lined the glory road to Boston. Glory Road because
Boston was the home of Fenway Park: the "jewel box,"
my father called it. That's what everybody called it, the
jewel box, a box that was crammed with emeralds
because everything at Fenway Park was green, green,
green. There was no advertising, nothing to detract from
the game and the color of summer.

Leaving my house we would have seen, as we would
have seen every morning that Boston was playing a home
game, a woman named Miss Kellogg waiting for the bus.
Miss Kellogg, a schoolteacher in her fifties, would travel
the seventeen miles to Union Station in Providence.

Then she would travel, by train, the forty miles to
Boston. Then, by hook or by crook but probably another
bus, she got to Fenway Park. Miss Kellogg was a real fan.
We all were, except for my grandfather, who adulated
the Yankees, and my sister, who adulated him. Together
they sat by his big radio, he with his right ear to its gothic
façade, and cheered on their team. If their team was
playing the Red Sox, we cast them into outer darkness.
Ours was a civil household, no plates crashed against the
walls. But we were serious about the Sox. The Red Sox
were ours as surely as if they'd been based at Guiteras
Field, up in back of the junior high, and my grandfather
and sister were incomprehensible to us. In casting their
lot with the Yankees they were turning their backs not
only on our team but on New England in general and
Rhode Island in particular. To Rhode Island we gave the
affection one gives the runt of the litter. We were
infatuated with its size; we thought our state adorable.
   It was also the best of all possible worlds in that,
though in a sense it had declared its independence from
Massachusetts centuries ago, Rhode Island had kept
Boston for its own. The Hub is less a nickname than it is
a fact; and the Sox belonged to us as much as they
belonged to Lynn, or Dorchester, or Southie. Why neither
my family, nor anyone else within earshot, ever evinced
a similar passion for the Braves I do not know. Perhaps it
had something to do with the National League. Perhaps
it was simply Ted Williams.
   Ted Williams was the first famous person I had ever
seen and, unlike every famous person (but one) that I
have seen since, he looked the part. Curiously, I have no
memories whatsoever of him at bat, only of him standing

alone in left field, as isolated by his celebrity as by his position. I don't recall his ever smiling or, for that matter, any expression crossing a face that was as soberly beautiful as Buster Keaton's. Today I flinch from photographs of a grinning Williams, fearing they'll efface my memory of that stern, solitary presence. His austerity precluded my ever having a crush on him, although I had just reached the age of falling in love with movie stars and he was handsomer than any of them. It would have been like having a crush on a monk.

I liked Bobby Doerr, too, as much for the solid thunk of his name as anything else. And Johnny Pesky's name, I figured, was what made him the scrambler that he was. As for Dom DiMaggio, a "little professor" was peculiarly suited to the Athens of America. Better yet, he was, my father claimed, the greatest of the DiMaggios even if it was his brother that got all the press. In fact Dom, standing for Boston, and Joe, standing for New York, symbolized the way in which we New Englanders defined the two cities. The one was class, the other mass.

Along the road to Boston my father pointed out landmarks from his personal, rather peculiar Baedeker. There was the diner where you could get the best buttered toast in the world, for instance, and the town that gave birth to America's plug-ugliest congressman. Above all there was the house on the Fenway, the house with the shamrocks carved into the shutters, in which lived James M. Curley, the former mayor of Boston. Like generations of New Englanders, my father had that weakness for scamps that made, and still makes, local politics a wonder of the universe—and that may explain the Red Sox' seemingly permanent place in local hearts.

It was when the car reached Commonwealth Avenue

and its squatty six-story apartment houses that Boston began for us: and at the Hotel Somerset that we finally pulled in. Our pregame lunch at the Somerset was why my sister and I were dressed for baseball as formally as we would have been for church. As my brother-in-law, who is still hanging on to his Jimmie Foxx–autographed baseball, says, "You had to look nice for the Somerset."

From the hotel it was only a short walk to Fenway Park. Boston is hot in summer, hotter even than New York, and our faces were red and our upper lips beaded with sweat by the time we reached our box. But not for long. The green, that all-enveloping green, acted like air-conditioning.

The Sox jogged onto the field . . . and it is here that the film freezes. In my mind's eye, Ted Williams is in left field, forever fixed in place. Maybe I looked at him too intensely; maybe I was as blinded by him as I would have been had I stared too long at the sun. I cannot see more. The reel doesn't start unwinding until we are back in the car, and heading for home. The sky is streaked with red now and the air slouching through the car's open windows seems exhausted by the heat. My sister, who is younger than I by eighteen months, has fallen asleep.

That was my summer of the Red Sox. It was, I believe, only one summer and to this day I cannot account for there not being more. It must have been Ted's entering the Navy, though, and my father traveling all the time during World War II. The trips to Boston ended, and my sister and I were pretty much stuck in our small town. She crouched in the bushes outside our house scanning the skies for Stukas; I kept an eye on the harbor and imagined periscopes.

Still, I kept up with the team—in Rhode Island, it

would have been impossible not to—and wept when Ted
married a woman named Doris. Too young for carnal
longings, and ignorant besides, I was made uneasy by
this capitulation to sexual affection. I was, in fact, like
the boys at the Saturday matinée who squirmed and
booed when it looked like the cowboy might kiss the
lady.

Through junior high and high school, I went on rooting
for the Red Sox but never went to another game. Even so,
I saw Ted Williams again, this time in a novel—in
Theodore Dreiser's *An American Tragedy.*

Charting the life and times of Ted Williams was a
constant preoccupation of the *Providence Journal* and
the tabloid *Boston Daily Record,* so just as I was aware of
Ted's having eyesight just this side of Superman's so I
also knew that his mother belonged to the Salvation
Army, and that he had spent part of his childhood
skulking behind a big bass drum as she, playing a cornet,
marched her family through San Diego. When I opened
An American Tragedy for the first time I was startled to
read something I was sure I had read before.

It is "Dusk—of a summer night," and a man carrying a
portable organ, a woman carrying a Bible and several
hymnals, and their three children are walking through
"the commercial heart of an American city." The man
sets down the organ, the boy sets down a camp-stool for
his older sister, the organist, and the mother says, "I
should think it might be nice to sing twenty-seven
tonight—'How Sweet the Balm of Jesus' Love.' . . .

"The boy moved restlessly from one foot to the other,
keeping his eyes down, and for the most part only half
singing. A tall and as yet slight figure, surmounted by an

interesting head and face—white skin, dark hair—he . . .
appeared indeed to resent and even to suffer from the
position in which he found himself." The boy is Clyde
Griffiths, as tragic a character as there is in American
fiction, and in his childhood he is Ted Williams to the
life.

Since Williams's mouth is legendarily foul, I should
not like to hear his response to so purely literary an
observation. But there it is. When Ted Williams wrote in
My Turn at Bat that "I was embarrassed about my home,
embarrassed that I never had quite as good clothes as
some of the kids, embarrassed that my mother was out in
the middle of the damn street all the time," he is the
young Clyde Griffiths lamenting that his family was
always "hard up," poorly dressed and "deprived of many
comforts and pleasures which seemed common enough
to others."

The famous, provided they are famous long enough to
become embedded in the public consciousness, are always hung with bits and pieces of their admirers' selves.
They become, in effect, armatures for dreams. My passion, and that is not too strong a word, for Ted Williams
was only partly informed by enthusiasm for the home
team and its most prominent player. Mostly it was fueled
by the imagination of a bookish little girl who saw in him
a Galahad incarnate. That, later, I saw in him the young
Clyde Griffiths made him even more magic. To me
Williams was human only when he opened his mouth
and confirmed—again and again—my conviction that
idols should seldom, if ever, speak.

Joe DiMaggio, on the other hand, was draped in love:
my sister's love for our grandfather. Joe was her hero

because he was his hero. If the Yankees were trailing, hopelessly trailing, and Joe had no more turns as bat, their hands would reach as one to turn off the radio.

It was on another hot morning that, years after the summer of the Red Sox, we set out for New York and Yankee Stadium and the treat of my sister's life. Bobby Feller was pitching against Joe DiMaggio and my father wanted us to see the contest. He wanted us to see everything there was to see in the world that we were soon to claim and that he was too soon to leave. He couldn't show us Chartres, he couldn't shepherd us across the Equator—those things we would have to do on our own—but, by God, he would, while he could, show us some great baseball. So we set forth, on a day that would melt marble, along the Merritt Parkway to Yankee Stadium.

We feared New York, feared it the minute my father told us to lock the car doors because we were entering the kind of neighborhood in which you had to be careful. This wasn't Commonwealth Avenue, these were slums whose blind windows were hung with limp curtains and slanted shades. Nor was this Fenway Park, this enormous stadium that had us climbing and climbing until our mother bade us stop because the heat and height were going to her head. This was everything I had ever heard about New York and its Yankees, this hugeness and this heat and, conversely, this chilling impersonality.

"Now I want you to watch the way Joe coils himself around the bat when he swings," my father said, joyous because New York was his town even if the Yankees were not his team. Yankee Stadium was no jewel box, but had we ever seen so many people in one place before? Of course we hadn't. We were shrinking to pin-dots.

As it was with Ted, so it was with Joe: I couldn't take my eyes off him either. Like Ted, he looked the part of a famous person. The isolation, the sense that he stood in a space that repelled invaders, was the same. But there was a difference. I could track Joe out of the outfield and into the batter's box. He got a hit off Bobby Feller, and he did indeed coil himself around the bat.

So now we had them. My sister had Joe and I had Ted, and we could both die happy because we had seen them in the flesh. "You musn't forget this day," my father said. "You musn't forget that you saw Joe DiMaggio *and* Bobby Feller." So we didn't, any more than we would have forgotten seeing Lee surrender to Grant, or David bean Goliath.

That was my last baseball game. My mother's, too, and my father's because he died the next year. Not my sister's: she kept it up, and she never deserted the Yankees. But it was not the last time I saw Joe DiMaggio. Once he passed me on Fifth Avenue, a tall, sallow man in a black raincoat, irrevocably separate from the crowd. "Guess who I saw today?" I crowed when I called my sister, jubilant because it was I, not she, who had nearly touched the hem of his garment. Thus, I said, is treachery rewarded. I hadn't forgotten how she cheered on the Yanks.

Now I watch baseball only on television, and only during those rare times when the Red Sox are in third place. Or in second. Or even in first. Then I wonder why I gave it up. I like this game; I like its lucidity. If I were to return, however, it would be out of nostalgia. Nostalgia is dangerous. If I followed the Red Sox long enough, before I knew it I'd be listening for "The Lone Ranger" and "Jack Armstrong, the All-American Boy."

I like to look at photographs of Ted Williams, though: so young, so gaunt, so terribly handsome. Sometimes I like to talk about him as well. A few years ago, for instance, I was reminiscing with a friend who was growing up in Boston at precisely the same time that I was growing up in Rhode Island. She sees me as having been permanently ensconced in the local library and I see her as permanently languishing in a swanboat or in a box at the old Opera House, so we were both surprised when we both confessed to having kept Ted Williams scrapbooks. We talked about his batting average and the Boudreau shift and of how the service gypped him of his greatest seasons and then she said it, the thing that all little New England girls, however far from puberty, said about Ted Williams. "My God," she said, "how I hated Doris!"

Pop Watts, a Newspaper, and a Day at the Polo Grounds

ROBERT W. CREAMER

There's a big difference between learning how to play baseball and becoming a baseball fan. I've known major league players who didn't know anything about the game, except how to play it. They'd heard of Babe Ruth and Ty Cobb, and maybe Lou Gehrig and a few other storied names, but that was about all. They weren't fans. The only relatively obscure player of the past that most of them knew anything about was Wally Pipp, the man who sat out one day with a headache and was replaced by Gehrig, who then played in 2,130 straight games while Pipp disappeared into the mist. Ballplayers know about Pipp because they worry that the same thing might happen to them—sit out one day and lose your job for good. But that's all they know about Wally Pipp. Dedicated fans know that he was a big-league first baseman for fifteen years and twice led the American League in hitting home runs.

I still see a friend I grew up with who was far and away

the best baseball player in our neighborhood. He could do things on the ballfield that I could only dream of doing, and he was still playing baseball in fast company long after I and most of our contemporaries had turned to softball. Yet after he stopped playing he retained only a cursory interest in the game, about on a level with my interest in football. I know who the best football players are and the top teams, I watch a few games casually on television during the regular season, and the postseason games with heightened interest, and that's it. I don't talk much about football. He doesn't talk much about baseball.

But I do. Like all baseball fans, I love talking baseball. I love to read about it. Wintertime sports pages without baseball seem arid and barren. A television or radio show on baseball always grabs me. If I pass a field where kids are playing Little League or high-school ball, or where three or four boys are hitting fungoes to one another, I'll stop and watch. I'm hooked on the game.

It wasn't that way in the beginning. I started playing baseball when I was about five or six, and I played the game for three years, or about a third of my young life, before I became a fan. Never mind Donald Hall's amiable guff about fathers playing catch with sons, as though taking a baseball in hand for the first time is a sacred rite of passage. In my neighborhood in the late 1920s baseball was just one more thing to do, like playing cowboys and Indians, or kick-the-can, or tag, or ring-a-levio. You learned to play it the same way you learned to play mumblety-peg or to rollerskate or ride a bike. You saw older kids doing it and you tried it yourself. There was no Little League. There were no organized, uniformed, adult-directed teams until you reached high school.

After you got a little better at throwing and catching and hitting you badgered older kids into letting you play in their pickup games. You stood near the foul lines pleading, "Gimme a game! Gimme a game!" If the teams were uneven (almost never were there nine on a team, and seldom more than four or five) the top players on each side might give in and let you play. If they did they might make a trade—in the middle of a game—to balance the quality of the sides: "You take the kid and we'll give you Johnny, and you give us Eddie."

If you were picked, you'd run to the outfield (you were always sent to the outfield), pound your fist into your glove (or, more often, into a glove a kid on the other team had left on the field when his team went in to bat), jump up and down a little, and yell, "Hit it to me, hit it to me," although you rather hoped they wouldn't.

While I was not yet a fan, I *was* playing baseball, although it wasn't baseball as kids playing Little League ball today know it. It was remarkably informal: there were no umpires, no coaches, no grown-ups at all, no uniforms, no bases on balls, no stealing, no catcher. Someone on the team at bat would retrieve pitches on the bounce and toss the ball back to the mound. There was a lot of democratic shouting and arguing ("I was safe!" "You were out!"), and special rules were made for the occasion ("Okay, grounders to the right side of second are foul balls; four fouls and you're out; pitch underhand to the little kid").

We kept track of the score, or at least had a continuing debate over it, but no one paid much attention to what inning it was, or how many innings had been played. Innings didn't matter. Games started if we felt like playing baseball and ended spontaneously if something more immediately interesting or imperative occurred. An ice-cream truck ringing its way up the street could stop a game cold. So could the discovery of a garter snake slithering through the outfield grass; everyone would gather around it, and someone would grab it and throw it at someone else, and things went on from there. Or a couple of kids waiting their turn at bat would start an impromptu standing-broad-jump competition in foul territory and soon everyone on both teams would be taking turns broad-jumping instead of playing ball. Often games ended in midinning when a mother shouted from a kitchen door for someone to come home *now*; a mother's commanding voice could be heard a pretty good distance in those quieter times before jets, helicopters, and power mowers.

In a cosmic sense, my early baseball years were a classic example of chaos—the confused state of primordial matter before the evolution of orderly forms. The precise moments of evolutionary change are hard to pin down, but I do know that my awareness that baseball had a form and a structure and a significance beyond that of kick-the-can and mumblety-peg began in our small backyard in 1931, the year I was nine. It happened one day when I was throwing a baseball against the back of O'Brien's garage and fielding the ball on the bounce. My grandfather was sitting on the back steps smoking his pipe.

I have to explain about my grandfather and his pipe. My mother called him Pop, and so did everyone else, but he was not one of those amiable Pops you see in the movies or on TV commercials, a genial, folksy old fellow who loved kids. Life had passed my grandfather by, and he resented it. He had owned a saloon for many years, but when he was in his early sixties Prohibition came in, and there went the saloon. He got a regular job then—people didn't retire in their sixties; there was no Social Security—but when he was in his seventies the Great Depression hit, and there went the job.

I remember him after that as a little old man with watery blue eyes and a crotchety temper. I don't remember him smiling. My wife, who as a girl lived down the street from us, says she was always scared of my grandfather, even though he never said anything to her. He never said much to anybody, although when he did it was usually succinct and to the point. When he lay dying a few years later three neighborhood women came to his small bedroom to say the rosary at his bedside, to pray, in the Catholic parlance, "for a speedy recovery or the grace of a happy death." My grandfather hadn't said anything at all for several days, but he heard the murmuring prayers, opened his eyes, and glared at the women.

"Get the hell out of here," he said. "Hold your damned wakes for me after I'm dead." As far as anyone knows, those were his last words.

Pop spent must of his time working down the cellar or puttering around the yard, generally minding his own business. My grandmother, on the other hand, was a positive, outspoken woman, readily given to telling people, particularly my grandfather, how they ought to behave. He liked rye whiskey and after he retired, so to speak, and was home all the time, my grandmother rationed him to a certain number of drinks each day. She'd let him have his first one late in the morning. She'd mix him a rye highball and if he were down the cellar or out in the yard she'd go to the door and sing out, "Pop, it's time!" Sometimes you could hear him mutter in reply, "Damn well right it's time. Damn old woman."

He also liked to smoke cigars, and my grandmother had some ideas about that, too, although it's hard to blame her. He smoked cheap cigars in an amber cigar holder, and he saved the butts and smoked them in a corncob pipe. The resultant smell was heady, and my grandmother insisted he do his smoking down the cellar or out in the yard.

I liked my grandfather—I still love the smell of cigar smoke—and I liked being around him, watching him planing wood in the cellar or transplanting flowers in the garden. But we didn't talk much. I mean, I never sat at his knee and listened to stories. He didn't explain carpentry or gardening to me, and I didn't ask him to. It was pretty much a silent partnership.

So this day, in the backyard, with me throwing baseballs against the garage, he was sitting silently on the back steps, smoking one of his cigar butts in his corncob pipe. Then, all of a sudden, uncharacteristically, he asked me a question.

"You like to play baseball?"

"Sure," I said.

"What position do you play?"

"Shortstop!" I said. It was wishful thinking. Only the best kids got to play shortstop, and I wasn't one of the best. I usually played first base. But shortstop was my dream.

"Shortstop," my grandfather said. "That's good. That's what I used to play."

I was stunned. You might think this memory is fanciful, but I lived in the same house with my grandfather for thirteen years, until his death, and except for his irascible last words and routine things like "Pass the sugar" and "Damn old woman," these are the only remarks I clearly and distinctly remember him saying. They made an impact. I even told my big brother later that day when he got home from high school; he was six years older than I, which is a lot when you're nine and your brother is fifteen, but I knew he'd be interested. I said, "Jerry, you know what? Pop used to play baseball! He was a short-stop." Jerry was impressed. "No kidding?" he said.

It struck me as so odd, so singular, that this grumpy little old man could have played baseball, could have played shortstop. Of course, he might have said, "You play tag? I used to play tag," and that would have impressed me, too. But he'd seen me play tag and other childhood diversions and hadn't said anything. Baseball obviously was different.

A short time later something else happened that solidified my growing realization that baseball transcended the ordinary and offered almost limitless variations on the splendid simplicity of its constant theme. The local newspaper that we read ran an anniversary edition, a salute to what used to be called the Gay Nineties, and reproduced in its entirety a page from an 1891 issue of the paper. One of the stories on that antique page was about baseball. The headline read, MOUNT VERNON ALL STARS DEFEAT WAKEFIELD 200, and there in the box score, sixth in the all-star lineup, was my grandfather's name: "Watts, ss." He had a base hit, too. My great-uncle John Brett played right field and had two hits, and their team won the game, 23–21. It wasn't until years later that I realized it must have been one of those jovial, keg-of-beer-at-third-base games. At the time all that I knew was: there's my grandfather *in a box score*. And that's when I became irrevocably hooked. Like the evolutionary fish that pulled itself once and for all onto dry land, I was now and forever a baseball fan, if still an embryonic one.

Then I found another newspaper. I was rooting around in the cellar for something when I uncovered a two-year-old Sunday sports section of the *New York Times*. I had only recently begun reading the sports pages, and to find an intact two-year-old Sunday sports section was for me what opening Tutankhamen's tomb must have been for an Egyptologist. The headlines said the Philadelphia Athletics had come from behind with ten runs in the seventh inning to beat the Chicago Cubs, 10–8, in the fourth game of the 1929 World Series.

My hands began to shake. I ran upstairs to find my brother or my father or my mother or anyone to show this extraordinary find to, and I was a bit nonplussed when no one reacted to it with the same astonished excitement I felt. To them, it was a two-year-old newspaper. Big deal. To me, it was ancient history. You have to remember that baseball in the larger sense meant nothing to me before that year. I was aware of Charles Lindbergh flying the Atlantic in 1927, the year I was five, but Babe Ruth hitting sixty homers that same year didn't register as much as a blip. Even though my big brother was an avid baseball fan, an avid Yankee fan, nothing that happened in major league baseball in 1927, 1928, 1929, or 1930 had made the slightest impression on me.

But now I was beginning to learn things. My brother kept a scrapbook of the baseball season, clipping photos and stories from the papers and pasting them into a school notebook he had preempted for the purpose. I read the scrapbook. I was reading the sports pages. I had started to read *Baseball* magazine. I was learning about the past. And here in my hand was a palpable piece of the past, a contemporary account of one of the most famous of all World Series games. No wonder that to this day I enjoy doing research into old newspapers.

The evolution was complete and my investiture as a full-fledged baseball fan was formally effected one Saturday when my brother abruptly decided to take me to a major league game. The Yankees were out of town, so he took me to the Polo Grounds to see the New York Giants play the Brooklyn Dodgers, or Robins, as they were called then. We walked half a mile from our home to the local railroad station, caught a train to Fordham in the Bronx, walked up Fordham Road and took a subway down to a stop near the Polo Grounds.

What I remember most about that fabulous journey was the subway ride. The car was crowded, and my brother was afraid that if we sat down we wouldn't be able to get off at our stop. He decided it would be better if we stood up near the door, and he held my hand to keep me close to him. But the Giants and Brooklyn were playing a doubleheader that day, and it seemed as though everybody in New York was going to the Polo Grounds. At every stop hordes of people pushed their way into the car and jammed between my brother and me until, even though I was still holding his hand, I literally could no longer see him. I don't remember feeling scared, but I do recall looking up from my nine-year-old height at the high canyon walls of chests and shoulders and heads towering above me. I remember a man looking down at me from that vast height and smiling with amusement. My brother kept trying to work us closer to the door so that we'd be able to get out at our station, but he needn't have worried. When the doors opened at the Polo Grounds stop the crowd surged out like water through a broken dam, and we went with the flow.

Inside the Polo Grounds we managed to find seats in the upper deck in right field. I saw the twin bleachers on either side of the clubhouse in dead center field, straight sections that connected the curved double-decked wings of the grandstand, and I wondered where the outfield rope used to be. My father had told me about the rope. His older brother, Arthur, was a very good second baseman, he said, and, according to my father, once had a tryout with the Giants. That was in the early 1900s when John McGraw was first managing in New York, and as I grew older and heard more stories it seemed to me that every other man of my father's generation had once had a "tryout with the Giants."

Nonetheless, that impressed me, although there was another story about Uncle Arthur and the Polo Grounds that pleased me even more. My father's father, my grandfather Christopher Creamer, who died before I was born, was a blacksmith who ran a livery stable on East 77th Street in Manhattan. One day when he was in his teens Uncle Arthur borrowed a horse and a two-wheeled rig from the livery stable and rode up to the Polo Grounds at West 155th Street to watch the Giants play. The grandstand at that time extended along the foul lines, but center field was open. It wasn't even fenced. Instead, a rope to keep spectators off the playing field was stretched across the far reaches of the outfield from left field to right.

Uncle Arthur reached the Polo Grounds and, as was common practice, tied the horse and rig to the outfield rope before going off to sit in the stands. During the game someone hit a terrific clout that went past the outfielders, past the rope, and into Uncle Arthur's horse, which reared up in fright and fell against the rig, breaking one of the wheels. Uncle Arthur had to walk all the way back down to East 77th Street holding the broken wheel off the ground with one hand while guiding the horse with the reins held in the other.

That old grandstand burned to the ground in the spring of 1911. My stepmother—my mother died in 1932 and my father remarried four years later—told me that her family lived on Coogan's Bluff, the steep cliff that rose directly behind the home-plate end of the Polo Grounds. When the grandstand caught fire, everyone living on Coogan's Bluff gathered at the edge of the cliff to gaze down on the burning ballpark. My stepmother said, with admirable candor and honesty, "It was one of the most beautiful things I've ever seen in my life. The rows of wooden seats were burning in curving, parallel lines. They looked like strings of diamond necklaces. We stood there all night watching it."

The ballpark, redesigned to enclose the entire field, was quickly rebuilt, and twenty years later there I was, sitting in the upper right-field stands with my brother. The angle of the upper-deck overhang was such that we were unable to see that part of the outfield directly below us, and all I could see of the right fielder was his head.

"See that guy?" my brother said, referring to the head. "You know who that is?"

I shook my head.

"Babe Herman!" my brother said, and things began clicking into place. I had heard of Brooklyn's famous Babe Herman. My brother pointed out John McGraw, white-haired now but still managing the Giants, and Uncle Wilbert Robinson, the Robins' fat manager. When a right-hander named Jack Quinn came in to pitch for Brooklyn in relief my brother told me he was forty-seven years old—older than our father!—and the oldest player in the major leagues.

Oh, that was a wonderful day. I saw Bill Terry, the Giants' first baseman, make a graceful unassisted double play. I saw an enormous right-handed hitting rookie catcher named Ernie Lombardi pinch-hit for Brooklyn. I saw Fat Freddie Fitzsimmons, the Giants' pitcher, who spun all the way around and turned his back to the batter when he wound up. When Fitzsimmons came to bat he hit a hard line drive that the opposing pitcher caught with a lucky upward stab of his glove, and I remember Fitzsimmons staring dumfounded at the pitcher, who put his head back and laughed. Later in the same game Fitzsimmons hit a home run to left field, and now no one ever had to tell *me* that Freddie Fitzsimmons was a good hitting pitcher.

I can't remember if one team swept both games or if the doubleheader was split. It didn't seem to matter. I wasn't rooting for either the Giants or the Dodgers. All I was doing was absorbing the wonder of major league baseball, inning after inning, sucking in details that have never left me. I think I am correct in saying that I adored—not loved, but adored, as though they were gods—every man on that altar of a field.

I didn't realize how sacred they were to me until just a

year or two ago, when I was looking through *The Baseball Encyclopedia* with a much younger sportswriter who has a fondness for odd baseball names—Carden Gillenwater, Baby Doll Jacobson, Ginger Beaumont, you know the kind I mean. He came across *Watty Clark* and laughed delightedly.

"Watty Clark!" he all but gloated. "What a name!"

I felt a distinct sense of shock. I enjoy the odd old names, too, but I didn't think Watty Clark was a funny name at all. Watty Clark was Brooklyn's starting pitcher in the first game of that doubleheader my brother took me to. You don't laugh at gods.

Coming to Baseball
. . . but Not Necessarily Being
Loved Back

FRANK DEFORD

Once I had a very acerbic agent, and one day, when she was either very pleased with me or very peeved at me, one or the other, I forget which, she announced to me: "Deford, you are the last of the tall, male Wasp, heterosexual Ivy League writers."

I suspect that was true. But, luckily for me, all those fortunate, blessed, snotty majority credentials were balanced out by the one quality the agent wasn't aware of, because she didn't know baseball. That is, that I also was bush. I grew up as a devoted fan of the minor league, Triple A, International League Baltimore Orioles, and as much as I resented that I was born to this, and thought it was terribly unfair, it was important in forming me and humbling me. Being bush is what obliged me to pull myself up by my own bootstraps.

I'm sure I would have been a lesser, different person altogether if I had grown up in a major league city, even one like Boston or Chicago, where the home teams always get beat. Big deal. This is a cross to bear?—you get beat occasionally in a World Series. Tell me about it down in Triple A, with my little pink nose pressed up against the window pane.

Anybody can love major league. I loved baseball. Even bush, I learned to love it. My love was gen-u-wine.

Also, I was very lucky in another way. Most kids come to a team when the team is already fully formed; it's like getting a crush on an older girl who already looks altogether like a girl. That's easy. Me and the Orioles, we grew up together, sharing a life. When I found the Orioles they were bush league. They moved to the majors in '54, when I was in puberty; that was the year I got my driver's license. We arrived big-time together. But it was still a struggle—*develop* is the word they prefer in baseball, and it is also a clever euphemism at the Defords' house, where everybody seems to take a while longer—and it wasn't till '61 that the Orioles came to flower.

That was my last summer in Baltimore. I was moving on. The Flock almost won the flag that year. They took ninety-five games, and but for Mantle and Maris busting 115 circuit clouts, the Birds would have taken it all. A man known as the Wizard of Waxahachie (his square name was Paul Richards) had brought the Orioles to the edge. They had developed, and so had I, and now we both had to figure where to go from here.

The Orioles won their first pennant and World Series in '66, right after I got married, and the next time they won was the year my first child was born. It was as if the arc of my life rainbowed with the Orioles. And since then we've both, the Orioles and I, won some and lost some, and we've grown up and changed owners and neither one of us has to be quite as important to the other anymore.

Back in the beginning, though, it mattered a great deal. Baseball is every day, utterly quotidian, and, as everybody who has ever read any soupy diamond lyric poetry knows, baseball flows with the calendar, too. It has rhythm, a sort of geometric rhythm, as a matter of fact, and it is green and timeless, sort of a timeless green, and if you'll stay here and buy me another beer, I'll also explain how the designated hitter has personally fucked up the Supreme Court and killed all the dinosaurs, too. On the other hand, make no mistake whatsoever that a team in baseball, a *club*, matters much more than it does in other sports where each and every team is only a team, except maybe when it is a franchise. No matter how much you might play baseball as a boy, no matter how much you chuck the old horsehide around, nobody ever comes to baseball without coming through the love of a baseball club.

Football and basketball are different. You play a little game of touch or H-O-R-S-E whether or not you really love a team. With baseball, it's more of a connection. Baseball is like the train going by in the night and the whistle blowing, and the little boy is lying in bed and he thinks of how the train is going to all sorts of wonderful, mysterious places in the world. And you would see the standings, every day, and they would read: New York, Detroit, Boston, Cleveland, Philadelphia, Chicago, Washington, St. Louis, and it was the most evocative train schedule ever printed.

And it was altogether unfair that Baltimore wasn't listed on that schedule. Baltimore was then the seventh-largest city in the nation—the *sixth* after it passed

Cleveland in the 1950 census!—and it simply made no sense to me that Cincinnati and Pittsburgh and St. Louis—St. Louis with two teams, yet—should be big league and my bigger city should be bush. I can't tell you how much this ate at me. It was anti-American. It was like if Idaho had sixteen votes in the House of Representatives and Pennsylvania only had five. All the other stuff God had been so nice to give me—white maleness in a white male world, heterosexual inclinations and Ivy League pretensions—all paled before the fact that I was bush. *Ich bin ein busher.*

Not only that . . .

Not only that, but . . .

Not only that, but what is your own earliest memory in life? Whatever it is, I'm positive it's not my earliest memory, which is that the baseball park in town burned down. Oriole Park went up in flames one night. It was not far from where I lived, down off the York Road, and while it was still smoldering the next day, my mother put me in the car, and even though it cost some rationed gas, she drove me over and we inspected a charred Oriole Park. Technically, that was my introduction to the National Pastime. It remains my earliest memory. My second and third and fourth memories are: V-E Day, Iwo Jima, and V-J Day.

Of course, even as impressive, forever, as Oriole Park was, burnt, to me as a five-year-old, I didn't know yet that we/I were bush.

That came a few years later, after the war, when I discovered the team, the club. I can still remember the names of many of the Oriole players. Ray Poat was the best pitcher. Howie Moss was a slugger, known as

Howitzer Howie, a leftover nickname from the war. Joe
Mellendick. Bob Kuzava. Bobby Young. Soupy Campbell
(I assumed he was the first and only Soupy Campbell, and
thought that was terribly clever of us). Al Cihocki. He
and Bob Repass were the keystone combination. "Hey
Bob, a Re-pass," us with-it fans would holler, after a
popular song of the time that went "Hey, bob, a re-bob."
I liked Repass, at shortstop, a little more than Cihocki, at
second, probably because Repass was rangier, and I could
already see that I was going to be rangy, too, rangy being
an attractive synonym for skinny. This is why, when
somebody asked me, What is your lucky number?, I
immediately answered: Six. Of course. That was Bob
Repass's number.

Ever since then, I've always wondered: how else do *other*
people decide what their lucky number is if they don't
have a favorite baseball player wearing one on his back?

The Oriole teams I loved unrequitedly were usually
good teams, only never real good teams. We never won.
Montreal invariably won the International League dia-
dem. The Royals were the gemstone of the Brooklyn
"farm system" and got all the good players. Jackie Robinson was sent to Montreal first. But I soldiered on and
was as devoted a fan of the Triple A Orioles as ever there
was. I read all about my heroes in the *Baltimore Sun* and
the *Evening Sun* and the *News-Post*. I would start to get
all tingly about baseball in February when at least one of
them would run the obligatory annual picture of the
steamer trunks being packed to go off to spring training.
Soon the pitchers and catchers would report, and then,
breathlessly, I would read: the pitchers are ahead of the
hitters. It was spring again! Most people think: if it is

spring, it is time for baseball. I grew up thinking: if it is baseball season, then it must be spring. Soon came the actual standings from the Grapefruit League, and the real standings would follow, and I'd finally hear my train whistle again.

Actually, there was a train that ran nearby our house. It was the Maryland and Pennsylvania Railroad, which we called the Ma and Pa Railroad, but I never recall hearing its whistle. Maybe it just didn't need one; the Ma and Pa never seemed to go very fast. It didn't have an Express or a Limited. But maybe I didn't hear any train whistle because, like most red-blooded American boys, when I lay in bed at night all my auditory components were fixed on the baseball game, which I was listening to on the radio which was hidden under my pillow.

The Oriole games were on W-I-T-H, 1230 on your dial (although I have not done justice to the W-I-T-H call letters here, inasmuch as there were not simple dashes between the W, I, T, and H, but lightning bolts). The away games, of course, had to be re-created. W-I-T-H could not afford to send an announcer to Jersey City, let alone to Montreal or Toronto, for bush-league games. But it was exciting all the same, getting the game from faraway Rochester exactly *as it happened*. Or anyway, nearly so. I was not, you understand, born yesterday. I understood that first what happened when Cihocki came to bat had to be tapped in by a Western Union operator, so that by the time Bill Dyer, the Voice of the Orioles, told me at home in bed at 6205 Mossway, Baltimore 12, Md., that Cihocki had grounded out to shortstop at Red Wings Stadium, Howitzer Howie Moss was already down oh-and-two in the count. Nevertheless.

Nevertheless, those were more innocent times and nearly live was quite good enough.

Bill Dyer, an old guy who was the Voice, had a gimmick that made it so transparent that we could all laugh along together. Every now and then, when the Orioles were behind and got a man or two on, Bill would say that, for luck, he was going to walk around his little red chair. We all understood that, in the studio, on the other end of the Western Union tapping, he was sitting in a little red chair. And wouldn't you know it, each and every time that Bill would walk around his little red chair, the Orioles would automatically follow up with a clutch hit or two. It never failed. Talk about telegraphing pitches. Talk about bush. We all knew that Bill was not going to say, "Now I'm going to walk around my little red chair for luck" if Western Union had already tapped it to him that Campbell had popped out and Mellendick had grounded into a twin killing.

Soon, at least in the escort of older neighborhood boys, I started going on streetcars to the Bird games, which were now being played at Memorial Stadium, a football field twisted into a ballyard after Oriole Park burned to a crisp. Bill Dyer's W-I-T-H radio booth was constructed right there, in the middle of the stands, up behind home plate, and whenever the Orioles got a rally going, all us wisenheimers would scream, Hey Bill, we need some luck, how about walking around your little red chair? But Bill Dyer was nobody's fool, and he would just smile and shake his head. He wouldn't dare do that unless he could be clairvoyant, like back in the studio for road games. And we would all laugh and jam our elbows into each other's ribs, because we were in on the joke.

They say it's the little things that win you baseball games. It's also the little things, different little things, that bring you into baseball and get you into the club, even if it is not the twenty-five-man *active* club roster.

Already, in fact, I was a Grade-A fan, which meant that I was serious about going to the Bird games and was not just going out with the hopes of snaring a foul ball. Nonetheless, I knew foul balls mattered, and I caught one once. It was fouled straight back over the screen by Carden Gillenwater of the Syracuse Chiefs, and I prized it at least until the Flock went into the big leagues.

I also began playing a card-and-dice game known as Home BaseBall, which was fairly sophisticated for its day and age. People try to get me in those Rotisserie leagues now, but I say, no, thank you very much, I did that sort of thing when I was eleven or twelve, only it was called Home BaseBall. It was a very private exercise. You could play by yourself, and in that sense it was sort of masturbatory, but it was safe sex; you didn't have to worry about hair growing on your palms with Home BaseBall.

But baseball helped me in life at large, too. Particularly it helped me in geography (which we have already discussed) and in arithmetic, since you had to know how to compute batting averages if you were any kind of a fan at all. Before I was out of grade school I could also work out earned-run averages, which is not easy (especially now), but which I could do in a breeze, even though I could never correctly change Fahrenheit to centigrade or the other way around. Unfortunately, nobody ever asked for earned-run averages on arithmetic tests, even though you might very well need that information some summer's day, say, between games of a twin bill. Instead,

they kept demanding that you change Fahrenheit into
centigrade even though in Baltimore c. 1950 nobody ever
did that, and, as an entire nation, we refuse to to this day.

And wait. I am not through with earned-run averages.
They are involved with this next part of my story, which
also has to do with young love. It involves one of the first
young ladies I got to second base with. (Now I'm up to
age fifteen or sixteen; I'm skipping around.)

(Also, before we get into this in particular, a telling
general digression: Inevitably, when people talk about
baseball and growing up, they always talk about how
pastoral it is and about fathers and sons and America and
apple pie, all that kind of *Field of Dreams* crap I ran by
you in the beginning, rhythms and timelessness, tra la,
tra la . . . *but* nobody ever makes even a passing reference
to the fact that the main point of reference about baseball
for most kids—even the kids who don't care about
baseball—is S-E-X.*

(Everybody knows this, but everybody leaves it out of
the nostalgic word pictures. But first base is kissing and
second base is feeling up top and third base is feeling
down below and a home run is what some other guy
allegedly gets. Poor old Jacques Barzun, who made the
mistake once of saying that anybody who wants to know
the heart and mind of America must first learn baseball,
and who has never been allowed to forget it, would have
been even more astute if he'd said, What does it tell us
about America that every kid in the U.S. who tries to get
a little nookie thinks about it strictly in baseball terms?
Heart and mind, my ass, Jacques.)

---

* These dashes are also lightning bolts.

But, anyway, here is Jacques Barzun getting into *Bart-lett's* about the same time I'm finally getting to second base with this teen queen. Or, I hasten to say in the interests of full disclosure, *outside* second base. I wasn't slugging any doubles off the wall, yet, just blooping them in down the line. And a little bit later, when the ardor had died down, this nubile object of my affection told me that not only was she an Oriole fan, which I already knew, but that she too could compute earned-run averages. And that just killed me. It destroyed me. It was so, so, so ungirllike. I don't think our relationship was ever the same again. I was just not interested in androgny at this time. Of course, this is not to say that I Stood On Principle, or anything drastic like that. I still kept groping for her titties, I still kept trying (unsuccessfully) to get to *inside* second base, but it was, emotionally, all over. My heart was on waivers, Valentine.

Now that I have talked about love and sex, not to mention arithmetic and geography, it is time for death and baseball. I had two deaths when it came to the diamond. One was a young catcher with the Orioles, a prospect named Bobby Lenn. He drowned one off-season, and it was in the *Sun*. Apart from a war veteran down the street named Angie DePanzano, who blew his brains out one Sunday afternoon, I had never really been forced to encounter death before. There must have been old people who had died on the fringes of my life, but old people are supposed to die, so that made no impression. And Angie DePanzano was supposed to still be crazy from the war. But Bobby Lenn just died one day.

And you know what bothered me the most? It was: imagine being good enough at baseball to make Triple A, with a shot at the big leagues, and you lose it all on account of a silly thing like drowning.

So Bobby Lenn's dying made a big impact on me, because now I had run across the irony of death, which is much more valuable to appreciate than the fragility of life.

Then the second death after I came to baseball was me, after a fashion.

I assumed, of course, that I would be a big-league ballplayer, and in preparation for this inevitability I began to master my game at an early age. I would stand on the front walk at 6205 Mossway, and I would hurl a lacrosse ball at the steps. Lacrosse was huge in Baltimore. Baltimore was big-league lacrosse, which was terrific, except, I found out fast, nobody else outside of Baltimore gave a damn about that. That rubbed in the fact that we were bush in what really counted even more. Here we were, big-league in lacrosse, and nobody else even knew lacrosse existed.

Notwithstanding where lacrosse stood in the national pecking order, though, a lacrosse ball is the best there is for bouncing back. A tennis ball is great for that too, but a tennis ball is awfully soft. We called tennis a "fairy sport." A lacrosse ball is every bit as hard as a baseball, but, unlike the old horsehide, it is made of rubber and it bounces. As a matter of fact, if a lacrosse ball comes off the steps just the right way, it kinda skids, just like a baseball on artificial turf. Of course, artificial turf hadn't been invented yet, so I was out ahead of the curve, fielding artificial-turf-type bounces before there was any artificial turf.

Unfortunately, this (as we used to say around my

block) and a nickel would get me a cup of coffee. Speaking coldly, objectively, I would assess myself as a moderately good fielder at fielding lacrosse balls bouncing back off the front steps. I wasn't even that good a fielder on a real baseball diamond where the ball took funny bounces. And also, I could field much better than I could hit. I could never hit with power, lacking, as I did then (and do now), power. I have always been bemused, hearing guys say they were fine in baseball, but then they couldn't hit the curve ball. I couldn't hit the straight ball. From Day One.

What made this even worse is that I wasn't just an all-around rotten athlete. Why, from the moment I first picked up a basketball, I was a pretty fair cager. Even in football, where I was brittle of body and courage, and didn't like to either (a) hit or (b) be hit,* I had, like, glue on my finger tips. I could catch any pigskin thrown my way. I coulda been a specialist. But baseball . . . baseball, my darling baseball, rejected me.

So, to rationalize, early on what I started saying was that I had "good hands." And good hands is a fine thing to possess, too—but only so long as you can boast of other things to start with. Good hands is only a fringe attribute in baseball, and in other sports. It is only meant to be ancillary, good hands. It is not something to primarily identify yourself with.

For example, here are some people who, metaphorically speaking, can be classified as having good hands in their line of work and not much else:

---

* Especially (b).

General George McClellan
LeRoy Nieman
Miss World
Neil Diamond
Fritz Mondale
Sir Walter Raleigh
Dr. Joyce Brothers
Pia Zadora
Davey Crockett
Eddie Cantor
Any anchorman
Billy Graham
Ponce de Leon

And so, as corny as this sounds, and I'm sorry about this, but it's absolutely true: just as Bobby Lenn's drowning taught me a valuable lesson about Life at Large, so did my inability to play good baseball instruct me about me. It is one thing to be born in a bush town, as I was, because that is not your own doing. But when you discover that you're bush entirely on your own merit at virtually the first thing that matters to you, you learn quickly to accommodate. I guess I started by learning how to compute earned-run averages.

I suppose most guys don't suffer a real loss of love until they're teeners, but baseball spurned me when I was much younger, and that was crucial to me, because it made up for all the advantages I'd been born with and helped me get on with life in a more sympathetic fashion.

It gave me a lucky number, too, and a sense of belonging.

Win Some, Lose Some

RON FIMRITE

In the summer of 1941, when I was ten, my family moved from the then remote village of Manor in Marin County to the city of Oakland across San Francisco Bay. That, I thought back then, was the second-worst thing that ever happened to me. Manor, an unincorporated suburb of the not-much-bigger town of Fairfax, seemed to me conceived expressly for the amusement of small boys. We—my mother and father and I and for a short time my teenage aunt, Fern—lived in a flat above a grocery store, whose owner, a merry Italian man, gave me and my friends licorice sticks whenever we wanted them, which was virtually all the time. A creek ran through the village which we sailed as pretend privateers on a makeshift raft. We sword-fought with Errol Flynn elán, using tree branches for sabers, and we scaled a forested hillock nearby which we called "Rock Mountain." Manor had everything I wanted in this world, and to be wrested so abruptly from my idyll there was a torment from which

I believed I would never recover. My father's argument that we were leaving because he would have a better job in Oakland and we would therefore have more money was, as far as I was concerned, made out of whole cloth. My life was over. Again.

Indeed, as I've said, the move across the Bay, devastating though it may have been, was merely the second-worst thing to strike me down. The hands-down champion worst was having to wear glasses, a torture imposed upon me only two years earlier by mean-spirited eye doctors. Overnight, I became a freak. In the mirror I could see that my otherwise flawless eight-year-old face had been hideously disfigured by wire-rimmed spectacles. Nobody else in the Fairfax Grammar School, except for a few aged teachers, wore glasses. Nobody in the whole world, as far as I could see, wore glasses back then. As a minority group all my own, I was subjected to cruel taunts of "Four eyes, four eyes." And I knew that both my athletic career and my love life were finished. In fact, the pig-tailed Sylvia Simpson, whom I adored, was conspicuous among my tormentors. "Perfessor," she called me. Perhaps I was doomed, as she seemed to suggest, to the life of a bookworm. Either that, or I could live as a hermit sharing my cave with wild animals on Rock Mountain. The fact that I could actually see better was of no consolation.

In time, however, my odd appearance was, if not completely accepted, at least tolerated by my schoolmates, and I learned to live with my handicap. I was practically back to normal when the move to Oakland hit me right between my begoggled eyes. The timing could not have been worse. It was summer, after all, and school was out. I would have no way of making new friends, and as an only child I was deprived even of sibling companionship. I was condemned, I could see, to a summer of solitary confinement. At least, I thought, my debut in school as a four-eyed new kid would be postponed for a few months. I would have an entire summer to contemplate that dreaded event.

We moved into a small apartment in the Claremont district of Oakland, near the Berkeley border. We were, as my father happily advised us, "conveniently located." The Montgomery Ward—"Monkey Ward"—store where he worked in the tire department was only a few miles distant and the Peralta School where I would soon be humiliated was maybe a ten-minute walk from our building—"The Last Mile," I thought. I took a test walk to the school one day and watched from behind a chainlink fence as some boys my age played softball there. I could tell from the way they kidded around and mauled each other that they were all the closest of friends. None of them was wearing glasses. I never went back there again that whole summer.

What I mostly did in those first few weeks was stay home with my comic books and listen with my mother to Ma Perkins, Pepper Young's Family, Our Gal Sunday, Lorenzo Jones, Mary Marlin, Helen Trent, and all the other radio soap operas until it was time, late in the afternoon, for Jack Armstrong, Captain Midnight, and Little Orphan Annie. At least once every afternoon my mother and I either played Chinese Checkers or worked unsuccessfully on experiments from my Gilbert's Chemistry Set. Sometimes we would all go to movies together and on weekends I was often left in the custody of a baby sitter while my parents went out drinking and dancing with my uncle Bob and aunt Lois.

As you can surmise from this regimen, I spent more time with my mother than most ten-year-old boys do. She was the buffer between me and total desolation, and it couldn't have been easy for her, because she was a nervous, hyperactive woman, then only in her early thirties. There was a fairly big city out there for her to play in—and a much bigger and more sophisticated one just across the bridge—but she was stuck at home with a lonely little kid.

My mother and my father, whose birthdays were just two days apart, grew up together in the small city of Minot, North Dakota. My mother, Mildred, or "Millie," was the elder daughter of Dr. Edward Ransom, the most popular doctor in town and founder of the clinic that bore his name. My father, Lester, came from the wrong side of the tracks, where the Scandinavians lived as the only real minority in town. His father, a Norwegian immigrant, deserted his wife and six kids when my father, the oldest, was fifteen. From that point on, Lester Fimrite pretty much supported the family, laboring at odd jobs through his school years and while apprenticing as a road surveyor. He met and fell in love with my mother, Minot's version of high society, when they were in high school. She returned his love with a passion that took him aback. She was just twenty-one and unmarried when she became pregnant with me. My grandfather, the doctor, gave the young sinners a proper wedding and then shipped them off to California to have me without further scandal. Even though she was later reconciled with her father and though he and my father became fast friends, I don't think my mother ever got over the feeling that she had shamed her beloved "papa." And I can't for the life of me see how this rather fragile and certainly spoiled young woman ever survived the poverty thrust upon her by the Great Depression. Obviously, she was a lot stronger than she ever looked or acted.

Nervous and even disagreeable as she could sometimes be, she was the soul of kindness and consideration for me in the first weeks of that summer of 1941. She was not only my best friend, she was my only friend. I was becoming, as my father and my uncle Bob observed with mounting alarm, a mama's boy. It was then that baseball came to the rescue.

Living in deepest Marin county, I'd never paid much attention to the game before. Oh, I'd played some softball at school, where, incidentally, one of my friends, Karl Olson, first developed the skills that would eventually take him to the Boston Red Sox. But I was by no measure a fan. I'd heard about somebody named DiMaggio, but I had no real idea then who he was or what he did that got people so exercised. That certainly changed soon enough.

I suspect it was my uncle Bob's idea that he and my father should take me to one of the ball games they went to almost every weekend and some week nights. Bob was born and raised in Berkeley and was a graduate of the University of California there. And from the time he was a small boy, he had been a fanatical follower of both Cal football and the Oakland Oaks of the Pacific Coast League. My father had played some semipro baseball in North Dakota and I'm certain he wanted his only son to be a ballplayer of some sort. But until that summer I had exhibited neither the talent nor the inclination to gratify that wish. In fact, it was only with feigned enthusiasm that I accepted the invitation to join him and Uncle Bob at an Oaks game one Sunday in early July.

The Oakland Baseball Park, which was not in Oakland at all but in the neighboring town of Emeryville, first opened for business in 1913, and by 1941 it was already exhibiting signs of deterioration. There seemed to be loose boards everywhere and the green paint was peeling from the walls and seats. The capacity was then about eleven thousand (expanded after the war to thirteen thousand with the addition of bleachers in right field), which was about normal for a minor-league ballpark of that time. The central grandstand was at least partially covered with a roof behind home plate, and the press box—more of a coop, actually—was situated on top, just above the protective screen. Bleacher seats down the left- and right-field lines were separated by walkways from the grandstand. It was in these cheap seats that the gamblers functioned, accepting wagers on anything from balls and strikes calls to pitching changes. The playing field was symmetrical—325 feet down both the left- and right-field lines and about 400 to dead center—and the outfield fences, plastered with advertisements, were uniformly twenty feet high. The advantage, however, was to the right-handed hitter because a hard and cold wind blew in from right field off the Bay. The giant horns of the loudspeaker system stared out from atop the center-field fence like the eyes of Fitzgerald's Doctor T. J. Eckleburg, and before every game they blasted popular recordings, usually "The Beer Barrel Polka," at spectators shuffling to their seats.

I had never in my life seen anything quite so wonderful

as the Oakland Baseball Park. It was even better than the Golden Gate International Exposition on Treasure Island of the year before or the Tom Mix circus of several years before that. The Oaks then wore just about the gaudiest uniforms in organized baseball, all red and white and green, but I thought they looked even more roguish than Robin Hood's Merry Men. Then, as they trotted out to their positions, I saw something so extraordinary that I had to catch my breath: the shortstop, a lanky twenty-three-year-old rookie named Bill Rigney, was wearing glasses! And so, praise be, was the starting pitcher, Jack Salveson, and the first baseman, Cecil "Dynamite" Dunn! How could this possibly be? Four-eyed athletes? In fact, at least six of the players on the 1941 Oakland team—Rigney, Salveson, Dunn, catcher Billy Raimondi, pitcher Stanley Corbett, and outfielder Tony Firpo— wore glasses either in the field or at bat, a phenomenon that prompted *Oakland Tribune* baseball writer Lee Dunbar to comment, "I never saw so many guys on the same club wearing specs." I saw this as a revelation, a vindication.

I can't for the life of me recall how that baptismal game of mine turned out. I vaguely remember Rigney hitting a triple and Ernie "Hooks" Devaurs making a sensational one-handed catch in center. But I do know that from then on, I was hooked on baseball, an addict for life. The checker set and the chemistry beakers would be stowed for the summer and even Ma Perkins' multiple travails would be put on hold. I mercilessly nagged my father and uncle to take me to games, unaware that my mere presence effectively disrupted their postgame eating and drinking plans. In time, they even took me with them down to Dahlke's in downtown Oakland, where they'd knock back a few beers and I'd tie into a hot turkey sandwich.

At first, I knew only the names of the Oaks' players. And what names they were: Cotton Pippen, Hooks Devaurs, Doo Dat Gudat, Hugh Luby, Mel Duezabou, Dynamite Dunn, Mike Christoff, Ralph Buxton, and manager Johnny Vergez. Even the team owner, Victor "Cookie" DeVinzenzie, had a nickname. Then, as I learned more, I became aware of the equally magical names on the other seven Coast League clubs: Pard Ballou, Oggie Ogrodowski, Frenchy Uhalt, Jo-Jo White, Ferris Fain, Brooks Holder, Broadway Billy Schuster, Tricky Dick Gyselman, Ad Liska, Jigger Statz, Hub Kittle, Kewpie Dick Barrett, Ray Prim, Nanny Fernandez. I heard those names night after night on Dean Maddox's broadcasts of Oaks games on radio station KROW— "How d'ya like those apples, fans?" And from my learned uncle I discovered that many of these Coast Leaguers had once been big leaguers. Lefty O'Doul, manager of the despised San Francisco Seals, had won a couple of batting titles in the National League, and Pepper Martin, the Sacramento Solons' manager, had been a World Series hero with a team called the Gashouse Gang. Tony Lazzeri, then playing second base for the Seals, had been a member of Murderers' Row. Hollywood's Babe Herman had been a big hitter for Brooklyn's Daffiness Boys. Earl Averill of Seattle had broken Dizzy Dean's toe with a line drive in the All-Star Game. Jake Powell of the Seals had been a Washington Senator and Marv "Freck" Owen of Portland and Jo-Jo White of Seattle had been teammates on Detroit's championship teams of a few years back.

School may have been out, but I was getting a first-class education.

I became a faithful reader of the *Oakland Tribune*'s sports section, which was, in that pretelevision era, truly vast. The sports editor and lead columnist, Art Cohn, took Menckenesque pleasure in flaying rival scribes on the other Bay Area papers. Prescott Sullivan, an immensely popular columnist on the then dominant *San Francisco Examiner*, was, for the insolent Cohn, merely a "Westbay hack." Other columnists, in his acid view, never ever simply wrote their daily pieces, they instead "pontificated," "elucidated," or embraced their subjects with "Pythian zeal." Lou Nova, the heavyweight contender who practiced Yoga, was, for Cohn, "fistiana's Trilby." Franklin Street in Oakland, where the boxing crowd congregated, was "Bash Boulevard." Cohn called his column "The Cohning Tower," in frank imitation of Franklin P. Adams's "The Conning Tower," but he was such a facile stylist that, in the Bay Area at least, he was celebrated as an original. I, of course, scarcely understood a word he wrote, but I was among his most dedicated fans, and I truly grieved some seventeen years later when he, a Hollywood screenwriter by then, was killed in a plane crash with his friend, producer (and Elizabeth Taylor husband) Mike Todd.

Cohn I read first, then I would turn to the other columns: Dunbar's "The Bullpen," Alan Ward's "On Second Thought," and George Scherck's "Down the Stretch," which was mostly about horse racing but occasionally about baseball. My father had taught me to translate box scores, and I never skipped a game story. I was learning more about the English language from these cynical sportswriters than I ever learned in a classroom. And gradually, as my curiosity grew, I gravitated from the sports page to the rest of the newspaper. I read Li'l Abner and Big Chief Wahoo in the comics section, and I never missed one of John Hix's "Strange as It Seems" items, though I was informed by my elders that he was merely a second-string Robert Ripley. But how else would I have discovered that Louis XIV had been an amateur ballet dancer or that "an octopus converts its food to soup before eating"? You don't pick up stuff like that in textbooks.

My father seemed terribly upset by the war then raging in Europe, but from my vantage point it seemed like just another sports event, with the good guys (the Oaks) from Great Britain and Russia taking on the bad guys (Seals) from Germany. And those war maps looked to me like box scores. Pearl Harbor later that year did little to divert me from this skewed world view; the way I saw it, we had just hooked up with the good guys team and the game would soon be over.

It was altogether an unusual time for me. A summer I had expected to drag on for an eternity had passed in a flash. By September, I had become an informed and ardent fan of the Oakland Oaks, a fanatic capable of reciting batting averages on command and quoting, albeit without full comprehension, the daily pensées of Art Cohn. And I could spell Czechoslovakia.

I was now for the first time in my short life absorbed in a world outside childhood. I had a passion. The Oaks could either make or ruin my day, so involved was I with the fluctuations of their season (they would, alas, finish sixth). I had heroes now who were flesh and blood and who even wore glasses. Superman and Batman were all well and good and so were the movies' Captain Blood and Robin Hood, but I could be there on the spot, rising out of one of those splintered wooden seats, when Dynamite Dunn—who "either struck out or hit a home run"— blasted one over the left-field fence with two on.

And though I made no new friends my own age that summer, I did reacquaint myself with an old one: my father. In Marin, where I dwelled in the company of other children, he had not played a big part in my life. He worked such long hours he wasn't even around the house much, and when he did come home, he seemed preoccupied, as well he might have been, considering our treacherous finances. And the threat, "Wait 'till your father gets home," did little to endear him to me. No, there I had my buddies, my creek, and my mountain. And my imagination. Always, for comfort and reassurance, I had my mother. When that famous summer began, she was just about all I had. But when baseball entered my life, so did my father. Now, when he came home from work, we played catch out back and after dinner we listened to Dean Maddox together.

Absorbed as I had become in my new life, I was oblivious to the breakdown of the old one. I did not see that in finding baseball and, in ways I could not fully understand, myself, and in rediscovering my father, I had abandoned someone else, someone acutely sensitive to being abandoned. Maybe if my mother had been somehow stronger or more mature or less vulnerable, she would have made it through that summer unscathed by my defection. I didn't even know she was hurting until one night near summer's end.

My father and I had just come home from the ballpark and were recounting in wonder and delight the Oaks' narrow victory that night over the Seals when my mother came into the living room from washing dishes. She sat down without saying a word to take in what was, for her, an incomprehensible dialogue.

"Dad, did you see the way Rigney took that hit away from Fain?"

"Yeah, that was something, but I think we won because O'Doul left Ballou in too long. That's why we got to him in the ninth."

"Yeah, but . . ."

"Time for bed, young man," my mother interrupted.

"Aw, Mom. . . ."

She led me down the hall to my room in the back of the apartment. The walls above my bed were alive with photographs of Rigney, Dunn, Vergez, and the rest. I changed into my pajamas and went off to the bathroom, my mind still whirling with great catches and clutch hits. I was surprised when I returned to the bedroom to see my mother still sitting there, on my desk chair opposite the bed. I took off my glasses, gave her a cursory kiss, flicked off my bed lamp, and scrambled beneath the warm covers. I would dream, I knew, of Rigney's great stop off Fain. And then I heard her soft voice in the darkness.

"I've lost you, haven't I?"

"What?"

"Yes," she said, "you're no longer Mommy's little boy."

"Sure I am."

There was no fun in her laughter. "You're Daddy's boy

from now on. You're growing up. You're in a man's world. I've lost you."

She got up to leave, and as she reached for the door, I tried to say something to cheer her up.

"Aw, Mom, it's not like that. Really. I still love you. It's . . . it's only . . . aw, it's just baseball, that's all."

Well, maybe it was just baseball. Or maybe she was right. Maybe it was something else, like growing up. Or growing apart. Whatever had happened, I knew right then, as I lay there in my bed, that our lives could never again be the same.

George Selkirk's
Double in the Sixth

BLAIR FULLER

Was it for my eighth birthday—my ninth—that I asked my father—in January—to take me to a major league game? I was just beginning to play baseball, the game that my father had played so superlatively (so I believed) in school and college. I had to see how I would, eventually, perform.

We went to Yankee Stadium on a hot June day, and it was a far more thrilling experience than I had been able to imagine. The speed and accuracy of the throws, the sure-handedness of every catch, the fantastic ability of the hitters to connect with the blurs of pitches were incredible events, each one! And equally difficult for me to believe were the immensity of the playing field and the stands, and the huge, freely passionate crowd.

I was growing up in northern Westchester where, in the mid-1930's, the dairy farms had been becoming estates for the past twenty years, but where there still were pastures, herds of cows, and stands of forest. The sounds of the steam engines' whistles on the Harlem River Line trains which passed five miles away could often be heard at my house where voices, if raised, were electrifyingly hushed by my mother or her surrogates. Decorum ruled so smoothly and entirely that when, at the ballpark, a man sitting near us in the third-baseline box shouted at the player coming to bat that he was a no-good bum and added worse-sounding, unintelligible-to-me insults after the man had flied out—and no one reproached him for it, indeed those around the heckler clearly enjoyed it—I felt that I was experiencing another civilization from the one I knew. The reactions of the whole crowd as it rose to its feet when a grounder got through for a hit and groaned together at a close out call at first impressed on me my ignorance of the world.

The following morning at the breakfast table my father told me to read the *New York Times* account of the game, principally, no doubt, to get me to read something.

I was baffled. We had seen the game, what was the point of reading about it?

"Read it," he said. "You'll be surprised."

I resisted. Reading was difficult and slow for me. Perhaps I had "mirror vision." I tended to write certain letters backward no matter how many times I was shown my errors. One teacher had guessed that I was naturally left-handed since my right-handed writing was so tormented-looking, but I had done no better with my left. I had been kept at my desk during many school recesses to exercise my writing in the vain hope that it would become more legible.

My father asked me, "Who hit the double in the sixth

inning that knocked in the winning runs?" I shook my head. "You'll find out," he said.

George Selkirk had hit that double, and I found out far more than that. Reading, I not only saw Selkirk's swing for a second time, the ball flying down the right-field line, Selkirk's lightning, high-stepping run to second, the dust jumping up and hanging there, a puff of brown cloud, as he slid in, I also saw the second baseman turning his face up to the umpire and the umpire's arms shooting out in the call of safe—things which I must have seen when I'd been there but which I couldn't remember having noticed. As I read slowly down the column I saw the pitchers' extraordinary motions once again (without TV in the 1930s nothing had prepared me for the sight of a full windup), and a fly ball caught up against the fence by a leaping left fielder. By the time I'd got down to the box score my mind was teeming with recalled sights and sounds, and my father was headed for the commuter train. He promised to explain the box score's symbols and numbers to me later.

No children's books had had much meaning for me. Perhaps it was because my parents' occasional readings aloud to me and my sisters from *Ivanhoe* and other historical, presumably gripping, adventures had seemed to me so unreal. This was not, I think, because of the characters and actions described in the novels, but because of the strange, theatrical personas that my parents assumed as readers.

My father had had Massachusetts parents and normally spoke with a broad *a*, but in these performances he became so mellifluously anglicized and declaimed in a voice of such articulated elegance that I became fascinated with the unlikelihood of his being my parent. My mother's voice became strongly inflected, ranging from notes well below her normal tones to an unearthly falsetto used in the service, it almost always seemed, of indicating what she thought to be oddly picturesque or, above all, foolish details in what the characters were doing or saying. She would often pause to shake her head or wink or smile at us, looking for confirmation of her being rather wiser than the people in the story. Her making judgments as though she were involved in these exotic situations amazed me. I would try to imagine her among the characters in *Treasure Island*, say, and the vision would make me want to laugh. Sometimes I did laugh, mystifying and annoying her.

The reality of George Selkirk, on the other hand, and of Lou Gehrig and of all the others I had seen that day was beyond question in my mind.

So the American League became my first great "learning experience", although I often despaired of retaining everything in the *Times*'s reports, and was at first overwhelmed by the amount of information in the Sunday lists of all the major leaguers' averages and won and lost records. They took so much time! After all, I had to play baseball, too, and there were other activities, like school, that were required of me.

For my next birthday I asked my father to take me to a National League game. That meant the Giants, and if that game was not quite so great a turning point as the Yankees game, still, it was of lasting importance. I had by then discovered the annual *Who's Who in Baseball*, so I knew a lot about the players in advance, what to expect of them and what to look for. I knew who would be pitching from the *Times* of the day before and, as my great good luck would have it, I saw King Carl Hubbell go against Paul Derringer of the Cincinnati Reds (he was called "Oom Paul," a nickname which baffles me to this day). The Giants won the game, 4–2, as Hubbell went the distance and Bill Terry homered, but as it turned out it was the Cincinnati Reds who won my almost endless allegiance, not because of anything they did on the field, although Derringer pitched "gallantly"—that was sports-page prose of the time—but because I later asked my father if the name Cincinnati was an Indian name.

He sent me—sulking, no doubt—to the encyclopedia to find out. To this day the story of Cincinnatus, the retired Roman senator summoned from behind his plow to lead the Roman army in its defense of the city against a barbarian attack, who triumphed and then modestly re-retired to his farm, seems to me the most satisfying of heroic fables. I decided that any city that had named itself after him must to some extent share Cincinnatus's virtues, and that therefore I would be a Cincinnati fan. Giving the ball club my hopes for the pennant was an act of homage.

So began my education in the geography of the United States. Why was St. Louis called the "Gateway City"? Gateway to what? The answer involved the Mississippi River and New Orleans, Napoleon and the Louisiana Purchase. Why did sportswriters covering the games in Chicago often allude to the stockyards? This got me into meat packing, the national railroad system, homestead-ing in the West, the rancher-railroad interdependence and conflicts, Jesse James, and the Big Four.

No major league club was then located west of the

Mississippi or south of the Mason-Dixon Line. Although I understood that the nation's biggest cities were Eastern and Midwestern, this seemed wrong, given the leagues' names, and unfair. Most of the ballplayers came from the South or border states, and a lot from California, too, and they would never be able to play as major leaguers at or near their hometowns, except possibly in an off-season barnstorming game.

After my father left our house in September of the year that I was ten I began to follow the minor leagues as well, to the extent that I could. The *Times* did not print box scores of minor-league games, but they did run line scores of Triple A league games, and carried weekly standings of a number of Double A and A leagues, and from these and *Who's Who* I learned the leagues' and teams' names, and developed favorites among them, mostly on the basis of nicknames that appealed to me.

In this way the missing parts of America came alive. The San Francisco Seals were favorites of mine, and I also liked the idea of a ball club of "Angels"—the Los Angeles club in the Pacific Coast League. Those cities' names got me into Spanish saints, conquistadors, and Mexico. The unbelievably named Toledo Mudhens of the American Association got my affection. (I later learned that, earlier, Toledo had had a club in the Western League called the Swamp Angels—such a gift for naming in those days! Among others, the Swamp Angels had played against the Terre Haute Hottentots and the Grand Rapids Gold Bugs.)

I liked the Birmingham Barons and, even more, the New Orleans Pelicans of the Southern Association—I had looked up *pelican* in the encyclopedia and the bird's extraordinary look of ungainly wisdom had immediately won my support.

Nearest to me geographically, and perhaps best of the minor leagues, was the Triple A International League which had clubs in Newark and Jersey City, but also in Montreal—the Royals or Royales—and in Havana—the Sugar Kings. Cigar-box art depicting beautiful señoritas in tropical settings made the Sugar Kings my team, and they will be again when political sanity has returned and Havana returns to organized ball.

Meanwhile I was trying to play as much as I could, not only on my grammar-school team but in whatever pickup situations I could find. My nearest friend, Donald Mullaney, who lived only a quarter of a mile away, got his father's permission for us to scratch out an unmeasured, lopsided diamond in an area bordering a swamp on his property. Donald and I, and any person of any age or sex that we could persuade to join us, played one-o'-cat games there all summer. Our ambition was to play nine-to-a-side baseball, and twice, or perhaps once, we succeeded in involving eighteen people, if only for an inning or two. Discarded cushions were our bases, and most often we had only one ball, blackened by the waters of the swamp.

It was Donald who knew of our village team, the Bedford Farmers, who played Sunday games on a public-school field near the village green. I knew most of the Farmers by sight as a grocery clerk, a fireman, and so on, and it made my heart swell with pride that they were leading second, and more interesting, lives. The Farmers and the teams they played were semipro. Donations were solicited from the crowd by the bench warmers around the sixth inning of every game, but more coins than bills went into the outstretched caps. Two of the visiting teams were revelations to me.

One was a team apparently composed of Orthodox Jews, the House of David, from the Bronx. All of them, except for two substitutes in their teens, were bearded, and some had ringlets squeezing out of their caps by their ears. I had never seen their like, and at first found it difficult to believe that they would be able to play like normal men. They could, though, and their ordinary skills and weaknesses established their fascinatingly ordinary humanity.

The year was 1938, and I was eleven. While I was not yet a steady reader of the news pages I was aware of Crystal Night in Germany, when the Nazis had broken the windows of all the Jewish shops and many houses. I had seen pictures of Jews made to wear identifying armbands being publicly jeered at. That the House of David's shortstop–second base double-play combination was exceptionally agile and quick, that only two of their hitters could do much against the Farmers' hard-throwing right-hander, and that after a while infield chatter in a strange language was essentially as understandable as English—these things established feelings of brotherhood that made the Nazi persecution seem all the more bizarre and horrifying.

A few Sundays after the House of David game, an all-black team, the Stamford G.O.P., beat the Farmers with relative ease, something like 8–2. I suppose that I had been conditioned by "Amos 'n' Andy" radio shows and perhaps a Stepin Fetchit movie role, because what impressed me most was the G.O.P.'s seriousness. Their sidearm pitcher was all business, no smiles, and there was no joking on the bench when the G.O.P. was at bat. When the game was over they shook hands around in a gentlemanly way, and drove off in three overcrowded cars with something of the silent mystery of a diplomatic mission.

When I saw my father I asked him why there were no black ballplayers in professional baseball. Needless to say, neither he nor anyone could provide a satisfactory answer. I had stumbled onto "The American Dilemma"—my father suggested that I read a book of that title. The book was so thick and its language so formal that I soon abandoned it, but the title had made its point.

My father's life had quite radically changed and not for the better. There were no major league games for me in the next few years. My participation through the press, however, took a thrilling turn. The Cincinnati Reds, who had been perennially second division in the mid-1930s, had steadily improved as Derringer was joined on the pitching staff by new talent, Bucky Walters, especially. Ernie Lombardi and Frank McCormick gave the ball club great punch. As the team headed for the pennant in 1939 I noticed that almost all the clubs that I had favored in the minors had improved as well. The Pelicans and Seals, even the Mudhens had got out of the cellar!

For two seasons or more my fandom clearly accompanied more success than failure. The Reds not only won the pennant in 1940, they took the World Series, and if the minor-league clubs could not match that, they nonetheless were doing more winning than losing. I secretly—absolutely secretly—wondered if there were something magical about my rooting for a team. But after '41 the Reds went into a decline, the other clubs had mixed histories, and as the nation's manpower became increasingly absorbed into World War II not only did many teams experience disastrous changes of fortune, whole leagues disappeared. It was in those lean years that I recognized my own true fandom. I missed the crack of the bat, the slap of ball into glove, the umpires' strike calls. I would hear those sounds. I would replay George Selkirk's double.

In October 1945, a month or so after the war had ended with the signing of the surrender on the deck of the *Missouri*, I, then an eighteen-year-old seaman first class, watched a night game in San Diego between a team of major league all-stars, led by Bob Feller, and Satchel Paige's Negro all-stars, a team that included Jackie Robinson and Josh Gibson. The two great pitchers went six innings each, each of them giving up one run. The Fellers scored again off a reliever and won it, 2–1, in a swirl of fog, but the game had been so brilliantly and evenly contested that it seemed inevitable that blacks would play in the majors. I thought that this change, and other liberations like it, would be the war's true victory.

I last played ball as a second-string catcher and outfielder on the 1947 Harvard freshmen team. I wasn't terrific. I developed a chronically sore throwing arm in the course of the cold, wet season, and didn't get into the season's climactic game against Yale. I was depressed, and not just for a day. It looked like, and it was, the end of my playing career.

A little later, though, that summer, Brooklyn brought up Jackie Robinson and the color line—not just baseball's—was forever broken. And, hey, I had learned to read, hadn't I? Starting with the *Times* account of that first Yankee game I had learned to read well enough, and had read enough, to be accepted by Harvard. Perhaps, at Harvard, I could learn to write.

The Bonding

MARK HARRIS

The telephone rings. I know who it is. It is a chunky, powerful boy with a thick, bushy red-haired mustache and a name, Christy Ratherbiglongname, I can seldom remember, and when I remember it I can't pronounce it. He wants me to come out and play. He is nineteen years old and I am sixty-nine.

One of the things that made me a baseball fan is its democracy. Lines of snobbish distinction go down. (On the other hand, I was fifty-five years old before I ever played with a black teammate.) On the telephone Christy calls me Professor. On the ball field he calls me by my first name. Only on the phone or at the ball field do our lives intersect. Baseball is our *lingua franca*.

"Where?" I ask.

"Lafcadio Park," he says. "It's a trophy game."

"When?" I ask.

"Saturday," he says.

"What time?" I ask.

"Get there maybe half-past seven, seven-thirty," he

says, "give us time to warm up a little. Do you see what I'm saying?"

He needs me and I need him. He knows what I can do. I'd been recruited by Christy Ratherbiglongname at a senior citizens' game at Chaparral Park, in Scottsdale. He'd been driving by and he just happened to stop and watch. So he said. My impression is that he'd stopped deliberately to see what he could see, and I was the man he saw. He'd be able to count on me. Nobody wanted me but him. I'd be grateful to be his eleventh man. I'd show up for every game. I could punch singles through the infield. I could play right field, first base, pitch, coach.

He was a supremely energetic young man. He slept four hours a night whether he needed it or not. My wife once said she was pleased he was not a military person— he'd attack other countries out of restlessness. "If you come and and play with us," he said when he recruited me, "the church gives you a free T-shirt."

"I don't like playing at night," I said.

"We don't play at night," he said. This was absolutely false. The league I joined him in played half its winter games at night and *all* its summer games at night. But he knew that once I'd been bonded to the team I wouldn't mind his having lied. He had seen by my way of playing that I was longing to be bonded.

THIS sport I am talking about is an extremely popular variation of baseball called slow-pitch. The pitcher pitches an underhand arc. Strikes are determined by whether the ball in its arc lands on the plate. If the pitch does not land on the plate the umpire calls it a ball. A third-strike foul is out.

The ball is larger than a Florida grapefruit, smaller then an Arizona grapefruit. It is not a hard ball but it is not a soft ball either. The most endangered player is the pitcher, who is often struck by line drives. The distance to the plate is fifty feet. Infielders are often struck by bad-bouncing ground balls, frequently in the crotch, which is painful for the victim and inspires other players to offer bad jokes as consolation. It is a hitting game. A player seldom strikes out.

The bases are sixty-five feet apart, much less, of course, than a hardball diamond. The distance down the foul lines is usually well under three hundred feet. Players' batting averages are closer to .400 than .300. Although these are high-scoring games they move quickly. A nine-inning game seldom takes as long as ninety minutes.

Slow-pitch is an ideal game even for teams composed of combinations of skillful and unskillful players, male or female. In hundreds of schools and communities sponsoring "co-rec" slow-pitch leagues, women's participation is governed by local rules. Every team must field a specified number of women. More and more these days, of course, many women players play very well. Christy, in behalf of the Salt River Pentecost Bombers, led us into a male league. Thus we have no women players, although I have heard some of our players speak fondly of women.

2

I too was once the whip—

> So was I once myself a swinger of birches.
> And so I dream of going back to be.

—the Christy Ratherbiglongname of my team, pouring half my energy into the telephone, rounding up the guys, routing them out of bed, out of the house, rounding up our transportation, pleading with my players against their mothers' tying them up with dental appointments, music lessons, visits to their grandparents. Baseball was urgent. Its urgency addicted me. We needed to win every game. The urgency of baseball made me a fan. Every game was crucial. One might be casual about many other things in life, such as love, learning, literature, morals, ethics, politics, religion, and college entrance examinations, but baseball mattered. I hated those mothers.

My father took me to the first big-league baseball game of my life. I know that the place was the Polo Grounds, in New York, and the time must have been the summer of my sixth year. The immense expanse of the grass was awesome. The feats of the players were marvelous. For example, batters hit balls which seemed to fly so high and far they would never descend. Yet soon enough they descended into the hands of players waiting far out on the grass. Such a relationship in distance astonished me. I was breathless to observe that a ball should be struck by a man with a stick at one point of the vast universe, and be caught in a glove by a man far away at another.

I was entranced by one of the Giants outfielders. What a peculiar name he had! Ott. I see it yet in my memory of that day's scorecard, and often on the Hall of Fame fence at Candlestick Park in San Francisco. Such a name began to suggest to me the diversity of the world: nobody on our block in Mount Vernon, New York, was named Ott. Rosenbaum and Schwartzman, yes. Ott, no.

Thus baseball expanded my provincial world. Ott's

teammate Carl Hubbell was called the Meal Ticket. I had no idea what a meal ticket was. My mother put our meals on the table. The sportswriters offered thousands of figures of speech to amuse a boy who loved the way words could be slung all over the place in a billion combinations. Hubbell "hailed from" Carthage, Missouri. Ott was called Master Melvin. Bill Terry was Memphis Bill

Carthage? Missouri? Baseball introduced me to geography. The cities of the east were New York, Brooklyn, Boston, Philadelphia, Washington. The cities of the west were Cincinnati, St. Louis, Chicago, Pittsburgh, Detroit, and Cleveland. West of St. Louis lay the Rocky Mountains and China. My active sympathies for people who did not live near big-league cities were mingled with a certain contempt for their having got themselves in such a fix.

Baseball made a reading fan of me. I was introduced to the connection by my father's evening commuting companion, the *New York Sun*. On the front page of the *Sun* one night I saw a boisterous, effervescent player named Pepper Martin sliding home on his chest to score the winning run for the St. Louis Cardinals in a World Series game against the Philadelphia Athletics. For me, that was the night of the wedding of baseball and reading, two pleasures conjoined.

As my mind embraced the game, the game enlarged my mind. Baseball taught me things even adults approved. *The game is never over until the last man is out.* Teachers and family relations thought this was a good philosophy of life. They liked to hear me say such things.

For me, however, traits of good character, if I had them, had nothing especially in common with life, only with baseball. Certain things adults morally approved I found simply useful.

Consider arithmetic. Adults approved my sitting there doing arithmetic problems, but in fact those were not problems I was doing. They were batting averages. It never occurred to me that this skill I was acquiring for the purpose of following the game would serve me afterward for other purposes. These arts or skills were pleasures in themselves. It was all one unified endeavor, baseball and reading and geography and history and arithmetic and newspaper report. I became a fan of baseball because I had once glimpsed the green expanse of serenity, and because the game called upon me for all those other arts and skills which were play in themselves, no matter what teachers or other adults called them.

AS A BOY I adored Camp Secor in the summer, especially our baseball games. I remember a game we played on a ragged, stony field against a team of boys from another camp on the other side of the lake. Their field was pocked with cowflop. So was ours.

When the game was over we boys of Camp Secor piled into the truck that had brought us there. Our driver was Uncle Arnie Cohen, who was also our counselor, mentor, and nature teacher. Beside our truck Uncle Arnie was shaking hands good-bye with his counterpart uncle from the other camp. The moment remains in my head half a century later. The other uncle says to Uncle Arnie, "Who's that little brat of yours who . . . ?" That was me he meant. Uncle Arnie replied, "That kid eats and sleeps baseball." I was proud to be noticed in that honorable way.

Once when we returned from a game across the lake I tried to convey to the folks of our camp the impression that I had won the game all by myself. Uncle Arnie challenged my report. "Nobody wins a game all by himself. Nobody loses a game all by himself."

Uncle Arnie taught me the idea of team, celebrated bonding. I understood as time went by that nobody wins a game single-handed. That was the thing that made me a lover of baseball, the bonding with one's fellows, the possession of their confidence.

SOMEWHERE, some years in the past, I am playing my position. I think I am playing shortstop. Two men are out. The batter hits a pop fly. It should be mine. Everybody sees clearly that it is mine. I am under it. I gather it in. But even before I gather it in I feel around me my teammates begin to jog toward the bench. They know that I am going to catch that ball. They have confidence in me. They know what I can do. They know my skills side by side with my limitations, and I know theirs. We are bonded. Baseball was bonding.

UNCLE ARNIE also said, "In the field. Want that ball. Want that batter to hit the ball to you. Don't pray the batter hits it someplace else to save you disgrace. Pray that he hits it to *you.*"

"TWO HANDS for beginners." Of course it wasn't original with Uncle Arnie. I caught fly balls two-handed. I still do. Uncle Arnie and every school coach in the universe commanded boys to clap that bare hand over the ball in the pocket.

It's no longer the style. The modern one-handed style is casual, confident, and cool. No matter how critical the moment may be—the final out of a one-run game, let us say—the outfielder plays the fly ball one-handed. He is too proud for precaution, for safety, his peers would laugh at him if he required two hands to do the work of one. But I haven't been able to change with the style, and I'm not sure I care to. I appreciate the security of that old-fashioned second hand.

BASEBALL WAS my model for the good life. "When a poor American boy dreamed of escaping his grim life," David Halberstam has written in *Summer of '49*, "his fantasy probably involved becoming a professional baseball player."

My life was neither poor nor grim, but I had my necessities. One summer, when I was a boy at Camp Secor, I wrote my fantasy in lying letters to a friend back home whom I meant to wound with accounts of my own great good fortune. I have written about these letters elsewhere, but an account of them is relevant here, too. Fantasy and fandom were bred together. For me, to invent the richest possible dream was to weave it of the stuff of baseball. I could imagine no life more desirable than the life of a baseball player, the luxury of travel, hotels and chambermaids, worshipful girls, players' uniforms, natty umpires, and, perhaps above all, the strictly scheduled reliability of life, for baseball could be relied upon to be present and to be prompt like nothing else I

knew: if Cincinnati was to be at the Polo Grounds at 3:10
P.M. on August 12 *they were there.*

I do not know what name my mind gave to those
letters—*letters*, I suppose, although I knew that
letters were true and mine were not. Mine were
wholly lies, fiction, deceitful inventions created to
excite my friend's envy. At their core were descrip-
tions of an elaborate Inter-Camp Baseball League, in
which boys in the most elegant uniforms traveled
about like professionals.

Each camp (I wrote) was required to maintain a
perfectly barbered diamond and sparkling dressing
rooms. Oh yes. Each camp was required to supply
new, white baseballs—none of your old tattered,
ragged baseballs held together with black electric
tape. Umpires were to be formally attired. The
grandstands were spacious, girls pressed forward for
our autographs—how boring to be giving out my
autograph all day!

In spite of that hardship (I wrote) I enjoyed myself.
Saying this, I permitted a tone of world-weariness to
creep in. Some people might find this sort of thing
exciting, but I'd much rather be home with *him* all
summer on the good old baking streets and good old
rocky choke-dusted sandlots of Mount Vernon.
Sometimes in a letter I'd "correct" an "error" of an
earlier letter. I provided settings for the act of
composition: today I am writing to you on the train
between Camp Indian Pines and Camp Lakadaka.
Listen to the dumb thing that happened: on this trip
our clubhouse man packed our *home* uniforms in-

stead of our *travel* uniforms, ha ha, that's life, I
guess. Oh nuts, in this hotel the electric fans work
very poorly, the chambermaids are very slow. Rochester looks so much like Buffalo looks so much like
Syracuse looks like Troy like Utica it sure is boring
I sure look forward to getting home to school in
September. (Glad we don't play *through* September
like the big leagues.)

These letters were written on my cot at rest hour at
Camp Secor. We almost never left camp between the
first of July and the end of August, and when we did
it was to hike two or three miles with canteens slung
across our shoulders in order to justify our mothers'
having bought the canteens. My letters were mailed
by the most careful calculation, bearing in mind our
eight-day swing through Schenectady, complicated
by the tedious necessity of coming back through Albany to make up a washed-out game. My dates were
painstakingly computed. Thirty-one days hath July.
No Sunday baseball at certain church camps. Follow
the weather reports and allow for rain. Follow maps
for useful details: in Ogdensburg (I wrote) I picked up
some Canadian money, in Lockport some of the kids
went to see Niagara Falls falling, but I stayed in the
hotel resting my pulled muscle. I had never been to
Ogdensburg, never been to Lockport, never pulled a
muscle. Where I *was* was on my cot at rest hour at
Camp Secor on my way to becoming a novelist.

3

My back aches. I want to go lie down somewhere. I want
to call Christy and tell him I can't play ball with him any
longer. Kid, it's over. Do you see what I'm saying?

Saturday has come at last. It is Saturday dawn and my alarm clock wakes my wife, and my wife wakes me. "Why do you set it if you're not going to get up?" she asks. "That's not fair."

"Of course I'm getting up," and to prove it I cover my head with my pillow.

"You were sure out," she says.

Yes, I had slept deep. I'd had a little bedtime sedative to ease my back. "How's your back?" she asks, and I reply, it's OK, it's OK, but I don't really know how my back is. I won't know until my feet hit the floor. I don't really want to leave this bed, but I cannot disappoint Christy G., boy whip, who's expecting me, counting on me. Right at this moment I truly couldn't tell my wife or myself if I'm going to play ball today or if I'm going back to sleep.

But this is nothing new. This is how it was when I was a boy and my bruises from last week's game were raw and the scabs were still bloody wet and my mother said if I played ball unhealed like that I was inviting infection, infection would course through my body—"gangrene will set in"—the doctors would amputate my legs and that would be the end of baseball.

The day is cold. Even so, I swing myself out of bed. I am terribly stiff, I can hardly move. Even so, I know that I am going to play ball today. I am going to get loose. People advise: "Use it or lose it." I am going to play ball and might even play it well, might even win the game with a sharp ground ball sliced down the right side. That's my specialty. They play me to pull and I fool them.

Tonight I will not be able to believe the misery in which this day begins. But it has always been like that. Indeed, I quite retired from baseball on May 27, 1960: "I

played center field for Language Arts, against Social
Science. We lost, 7–1, my legs are unendurably stiff, & I
have the feeling this may be my last game. . . . Baseball is
for boys." So said my diary one day when I was only
thirty-seven and a half.

Baseball taught me to know I could rise to the occasion
(once I got out of bed). Baseball acquainted me with
my own resources, with the outer limits of my body. I
rise, I dress. I pull over my head my Salt River Pentecost Church T-shirt blazing blue bearing some sort
of design on the back I have never really identified. I
think it may be a box kite, though I don't know why it
should be.

Some of our T-shirts include the word Bombers. I don't
know whether the word is an addition to the shirt or
whether it had been there in the first place and was
removed as an ethical afterthought. I have never been to
the church for which I so faithfully play. I have never
seen it. I do not know where it is. I do not know anyone
who belongs to it except Christy Ratherbiglongname,
who alludes to it often as a checkpoint on his daily
rounds. But I have never heard any of our teammates
mention it. (In 1941, when I was employed in New York
by Paramount Pictures I played on the Paramount baseball team. I slowly discovered in my sweet innocence
that I was the only member of the team actually employed by Paramount.)

ONCE I TOLD Christy my best religious baseball joke, but
it offended him:

Two baseball players were lounging in their hotel room

one night. One player was a pitcher and the other was a third baseman. They began to talk about heaven. They wondered if baseball is played in heaven. They agreed that whichever of them died first would notify the survivor whether baseball is played in heaven.

The years passed. The third baseman died. He remembered his promise to communicate from heaven. He spoke through the spiritual ether to his old-time friend and teammate, the pitcher. He said, "You know, I promised to find out if baseball was played in heaven and let you know first thing, and I've done it just like I promised."

"I knew you would," the pitcher said. "What's the scoop?"

"Mixed," the third baseman said from heaven. "There's good news and bad news. Which do you want first?"

"Start with the good news," the pitcher said.

"The good news is," the third baseman said, "that we play baseball all the time on a regular schedule in heaven."

"And the bad news—" the pitcher asked from earth.

"The bad news is you're scheduled to pitch tomorrow."

Christy did not laugh. The funny part eluded him, violated his picture of reality. "Going to heaven can't be bad news," Christy said.

I DEVOUR half a grapefruit and a slice of toast and half a cup of coffee. Play first, eat a second breakfast with the Bombers later. Small breakfast digesting, I lower myself to the living-room floor. My wife leads me through a series of stretching exercises to prepare my back for the game.

I pack my equipment bag: glove, extra shoelaces, a small roll of adhesive tape, and my sturdy pair of Sport-goggle2.

When I leave the house I hurry. Apparently I am afraid of missing something. Butterflies flutter in my stomach. It was always true of me that I approached a baseball field, whether as player or as spectator, with a feeling of rising excitement, eager to be there early, fearful of something happening without me. Maybe I'm afraid of being left out, kicked off the team. "Late! You're off the team!" the tyrant manager shouts at me.

Full daylight now, dawn has dissolved, the temperature is forty degrees on a December morning in Tempe, Arizona, on the way to seventy, and the time is seven-twenty. I'll be at Lafcadio Park at seven-thirty, Christy will direct our warmup, and at eight o'clock we'll take on those Ball Crushers.

We'll beat them, too, I think. We have played them twice and they aren't much. These games are just fun, of course, but the fun is greater when we win than when we lose. When we lose we are filled with the necessity to apologize, to confess our errors as a way of emphasizing that they weren't the whole story, that it was the *team* that lost: our undoing was a collective enterprise. When we go for a second breakfast everything tastes better if we have won.

My car radio tells me the temperatures around the country. The wind-chill factor is forty-four degrees below zero in Minneapolis. I arrive at Lafcadio Park. I have hurried to get here. Christy will be there before me, ready to start our practice. He is persuaded that practice is the secret of our success, and I am inclined to agree with him. When we practice we start each of our games with a thirty-minute advantage. Our slothful opponents are never warmed up until the third or fourth inning, and by that time we have sunk them. They have lain in bed too long.

Nobody is here but me. I am standing swearing to myself in the cold at seven-forty in the morning at Lafcadio Park. Not alone the Ball Crushers but the Salt River Pentecost Church Bombers lie home in bed. To hell with this childish game. I am through with it forever. I quit. I will never get out of bed again. I will rest my aching back.

Since I'm here anyhow I'll run my back a little. I set my equipment bag on the player bench and jog across the grass. A humorist has planted a flag on a stick in a small mound of dogshit behind second base. The American national game is cowflop and dogshit, then and now, from Camp Secor in the Hudson Valley to the Arizona desert. This is the first time this morning I have smiled. I move stiffly. I feel awkward. I jog toward the left-field fence. I decide to jog another fifty paces and turn and break into a run. I imagine that just as I make my turn I will hear the roar of Christy's truck and the clamor of our team leaping to play.

I am warming. I am getting ready to play. I turn. Now I am running well and reasonably gracefully. I no longer feel awkward. My back is loose. The home stretching did good. I am grateful to my wife for her exercise leadership. The impossible has happened, as in bed I knew it would: my body has returned to me one more time. I will not hear from by back again until tomorrow.

But neither Christy's truck nor anything nor anyone

else has arrived. When I reach the player bench I am breathing hard, and for a moment the mass failure of Christy and my teammates strikes me as an event of no consequence. Indeed, they did me the greatest favor. If I had not got up to meet thcm here I would not have run, and if I had not run I would not feel as great as I do this minute. I pick up my equipment bag and drive home. By the time I arrive home I am damn mad.

My wife says, "There just must have been some misunderstanding." "There was no misunderstanding. It's the price I pay for playing with kids. They don't think. They don't keep track of things. They don't write their appointments down. They don't remember anything." "They're not all kids," my wife says. "I thought you had one other old guy." "We got one guy about forty," I say. "I call forty a kid."

I telephone Christy. I reach his machine, which blesses me and instructs me to leave my name and number and the time of my call. I say, "Christy, this is Mark, I just want you to know how damn mad I am, I just got back from Lafcadio Park, I was there at half past seven and I waited until eight and nobody came, so to hell with it after this, I'm just going to play with the seniors in Scottsdale, to hell with you and the Bombers."

I return to bed. I sleep for one hour. I rise. I read pages in two manuscripts in progress, one of mine and one of a student.

My wife and I walk in the neighborhood. On the golf course the gray-haired snowbirds from North Dakota, South Dakota, Montana, and Minnesota fire away. Golf must be a great gamc. You do not need eighteen people to play. "I'm going to take up golf," I say. "I doubt it," says my wife. We return home.

A message is on our machine. "Hi, Professor, this is Christy, got your message. The game is still at eight, we need you, be there at seven-thirty we can warm up. Do you see what I'm saying? It's a funny thing you went there this morning, trophy games are always night."

THE NIGHT is as cold as this morning was, without even this morning's prospect of warming. I wear a jacket during batting practice. I slash a couple of pitches to the left side. I made good contact. I like the sound. Right away I know that I am hitting well tonight. My hands sting in the cold. A teammate says I should buy myself batting gloves. In my generation batting gloves were unheard of, unthinkable. God did not intend us to wear gloves while batting—nor to bat with aluminum bats. I slash two or three more ground balls to the left side. I feel that they were hard-hit. I do not think the Ball Crushers' third baseman would have had an easy time handling them.

I jog to right field. If I play tonight that's where I'll play. I need to catch one fly ball for confidence. That will do it. However, none of my fellow Bombers hits anything in the air to me. We have only one left-handed batter, and he is a light hitter like me. He and I are the only players who have never hit a home run for the Bombers. (I have not hit a home run for *anybody* for nineteen years—I hit my last home run playing at the California Institute of the Arts in 1972.) He strokes two or three balls to right field but with only the force of singles. Playing them off the grass in no way assists my confidence—almost anybody can pick up a rolling ball.

As our practice ends, my alert boy Christy consider-

ately fungoes a couple of fly balls my way. The first ball
Christy hits to me I catch almost without moving a step.
For the second ball I backpedal a dozen steps to the fence,
and as the ball smacks the pocket of my glove my
confidence rises to its comfort level. Christy has done
just what I need. He knows my requirement for confidence. He is grateful to any player who shows up. I am
one of his faithful. I am ready to play.

Eleven Bombers are here tonight, and I see that I will
not start. "You'll get in," Christy says. "Stay warm and
coach third." We join him for prayer. Some time ago
when I told Christy I did not believe in God he said, "He
won't mind." We form a circle around him, we extend
our arms and clasp hands, we bow our heads, and Christy
prays. His red-haired bushy mustache quivers. "Dear
God, we sincerely love You and pray You will help us do
the right things when we play this game right now. We
know that You will keep us from doing anything we
don't want to be sorry for doing, and in Your mercy help
us show good sportsmanship to the adversary."

Our adversary is formed from a pool of discount-store
employees and United Parcel Service drivers and han-
dlers. We are a much better team than these Ball Crushers, and we are warm and they are cold. They have barely
made their way into trophy play. I expect a lot of traffic
to be coming my way at third base. I love it. I love waving
my teammates home. I am their guide and protector. I
also love halting them, keeping them safe. As they charge
at me from second base I cry, "Look at me, look at me,
look at me," and if they do as I say I will keep them from
harm. Some Bombers base runners sometimes defy me,
ignore my signals, charge past me, passionate to score,

and although I am first and last a devoted team person, I feel at such times a secret satisfaction at their getting their asses thrown out at the plate.

We score abundantly without delay. In the coaching box I am waving home so many of my mates that I heat up as if I were playing. We score ten runs in three innings. We are secure. We will never blow a ten-run lead. The Ball Crushers score once. We lead by 10–1. We lead by 11–4. We lead by 12–6.

After five innings our dependable shortstop must go home—not to home plate but home to his house. Our right fielder comes in to play shortstop, and I go to right field where I am instantly employed. The first Ball Crusher to come to bat hits a line drive to me. He is a right-handed batter. He had looked my way when he came to bat, and I knew he had it in mind to try out the old man. The ball begins to float, catching me unprepared. For a moment I am alarmed that I have misjudged it. I envision its sailing over my head. But I need only to rise on my toes and reach for it, and catch it in the pocket of my glove with a satisfying sound.

For some reason we Bombers cannot sustain the success with which we began, while the Ball Crushers begin to hit safely repeatedly. This is one of baseball's perpetual recurring mysteries: why does one player, one team, inexplicably lose its command, or another inexplicably exceed all expectations? The score is 12–8, then 13–11, and soon thereafter 13–all.

Nothing comes my way in the air. At bat I ground very hard to third base, but the Ball Crusher third baseman throws me out. When I come to bat again a Ball Crusher calls out, "Watch the line." The third baseman moves toward the line, and I think I can hit it past him to his left, but once again I ground to him. They've got my number. They've got me "defensed."

This is not to be believed. We are really a much better team than they are. They go ahead of us, 16–15.

In the top of the ninth inning when my mates are on the bases and everything depends on me, and all the Ball Crushers are playing me to the left, I punch the ball down the first-base side between the wide-playing baseman and the line. Nothing is lovelier to me than the sight of the ball I have hit skipping over the dirt to the outfield grass.

I had done it again. It was my specialty. More than once in a late inning I've whacked the ball just right through that wide-open space between the first baseman and his base. The Ball Crushers were playing me to pull —that is to say, to hit the ball in my natural direction, down the left-field side. They shifted to the left for me. The second baseman played almost on the bag. The first baseman played wide. The famous old logician said, "Hit it where they ain't," and so I did, and ran exalted to first base.

I am in paradise, I am praised by my mates. They say, "Hey, good job, man." Christy says, "You did a smart thing, I knew you'd do it." They all knew I would do it. They knew that my moment had come. It was the secret we shared together.

In right field, in the bottom half of the ninth inning, beneath the bright lights and the depths of the blackness beyond, in the cool night growing colder, in my exhilaration, my spirit glows with triumph. Through me the voice of Uncle Arnie speaks out of the past: "I want that ball. Hit it to me. Batter, hit that ball to me, I pray you hit it to me." Whereupon, with two Ball Crushers on base and two men out the batter does in fact hit it to me. It is a soft fly ball, spinning in the lights. I am under it. But even before I gather it in I feel around me my teammates unburdened of their tension. They know that I am going to catch that ball. They have confidence in me. They know what I can do.

I think I'll make a one-handed catch of it. I'll join the modern world, stick one hand up and allow that ball to settle in, which it does, and then pops out again and falls to the grass, while our adversary dashes across the plate with the winning run.

CHRISTY, almost as if he were not about to cry, rallied his men to his truck. He would not bring himself to look at me. Eliminated in the first round of trophy play! This was unspeakable. At last he looked at me and said, "You got your car, you don't need a ride. I'll give you a call." I always had my car. I never rode in his truck.

I WAS ABOUT to fall into depression. My worst moment would occur on the following morning, when I awoke to the dreadful memory of that ball's having popped out of my glove. It was a moment of my baseball life I will always want back. In the end I might deliver one of those oblique deathbed statements for which mildly eccentric men become famous: "I should have caught it two-handed."

But this is no fatal wound. It is a memory, not a traumatic incident. I am sustained by the truths I have learned from baseball. All the game's commonplace wisdom serves me. "You can be a hero one day and a goat the next." I was a hero in the top of the ninth and a goat in the bottom of the same inning.

"That's baseball."

"You can't win 'em all."

"People forget, tomorrow's a new ball game." I don't know about that. I don't think Christy has forgotten. He said he'd call. Where's his call? I'm waiting.

Everybody learns in her/his own way about losing. For me, baseball taught me losing and winning, taught me never to let anything get me too far down or too far up. You not only can't win 'em all—you can't win much more than half, hard as you try, long as you live.

Baseball was my path to self-knowledge. Baseball made me a fan by telling me truths about myself. It taught me to know what I can do and what I can't. I will make good plays and bad plays. Every so often the easiest pop fly is going to pop out of your glove. I don't care who you are. It's the iron statistics. It's fate. If baseball taught me—I heard it first from Uncle Arnie—that I don't win games single-handed, then neither do I lose them, either. *It takes a whole team to lose a ball game.* Hey, look, I didn't blow that ten-run lead all by myself, did I?

Here's Your Son, Mister, or How I Became a Baseball Fan

WILLIAM KENNEDY

I owned a rubber baseball, a glove, a bat, and a uniform at such an early age I can't know how young I was. I know from photographs that I was using them well before my precocity with spheres, diamonds, numbers, and letters allowed me to enter first grade at age five in 1933. My uncle Peter pitched to me on the front lawn, and my great aunt Lella caught the pitches I didn't hit. The glove was a pair of leather slabs without padding, and for catching a ball it was as practical as a tin plate.

By perhaps 1935 or 1936 the New Deal had come to North Albany, and the Rooseveltian minions in the Works Progress Administration were building tennis courts and leveling the huge open field behind Public School 20 (and next door to our house), where everybody played baseball and football and golf and where, Lou Pitnell tells me, he and I caught fly balls and grounders hit by the tall, thin, fiftyish foreman of the WPA gang, a man named Mac, while Mac's underlings cleared rocks, moved and raked dirt, planted grass, and beautified the sandlot where cows had grazed when this was a pasture on the Brady farm.

I've tried to dredge Mac up from memory but he's not even a phantasm. But I remember Lou Pitnell's glove from those days—very stiff leather but with a good pocket—and my own: a yellow first baseman's mitt that I still own, although the yellow is now mostly black, and the rawhide webbing has rotted. That glove was why I usually played first, even though I was a right-hander. Lou threw righty but batted lefty, something I never understood in people until I began to write about politics. Bob Burns, another sandlotter, remembers very few left-handed players—Billy Corbett, Billy Riedy—but no lefty pitchers whatever. Neither of us can explain this phenomenon.

If I don't remember Mac I do remember the other "older guys" who hit and caught fly balls and grounders ("hittin' 'em out" was the official name of this game)—a rollicking band of aging players who came out for exercise, and a communal reveling in the sport of their youth, many nights after supper when it wasn't raining.

There was my uncle Peter; and Andy Lawlor: tall, thin, saturnine, with a long-fingered glove that had no padding, and a heart ailment that allowed him to pitch but not hit or field ("Never run for a bus; let it go and catch the next one," his doctor told him); and his brothers Jim, John ("Knockout"), and Tommy ("Red"), Tommy a pepperpot shortstop who remembered his own sandlot days in Carroll's Field near the railroad tracks, owned by my great-grandfather, Big Jim Carroll. Tommy played in the Twilight League, the organized semipros, and Joe Mur-

phy played in the Class D Eastern Shore League (where
Jimmie Foxx came from), and John ("Bandy") Edmunds,
the man we all remember as North Albany's best player,
went up to play professionally but wouldn't wear a
uniform because of his bandy legs, and came back home
to work as a fireman.

But Bandy had no qualms about showing his legs when
he played behind School 20. He hit and fielded in his cap,
socks, spikes, and jock strap, caught long fly balls behind
his back, and then, with a whirl and a bullet throw back
to the hitter, he would announce: "There's only a few of
us left." Certain North Albany women conveyed to the
parish priest their outrage at Bandy's jock show, or so I've
been told—I can't remember this protest either—and
from then on Bandy had to play wearing trousers. What's
the free world coming to?

THE SCHOOL 20 field was where baseball began in my
head, my heart, my right arm—with the kids and with
the men. As kids alone we played pickup of any sort:
"Roll-y at the bat," which required you to field a fly and
then throw a grounder toward the bat lying on the
ground, and if you hit it you took over as fungo man; or
maybe, when it was one of those golden days, you could
round up two outfielders and three infielders for two
teams and have a game of sorts; or maybe even two full
squads for a *real* game, if it was a sunlit Saturday.

I was about eight when I started taking banjo lessons
from a local jazz guitarist and banjoist, Mike Pantone,
who was sometimes on time for the lesson, sometimes so
early that I was still playing ball; and so the very portly

Mike would dig in behind the plate and umpire for us till the game ended and the music began.

The organization of Little League teams, with managers, uniforms, a stadium, all the necessary equipment, was not even a likely dream for us. We often played with cracked bats and coverless balls whose interior string was held together by black tape. The diamond was in three different places—the first where Mac and his men had put it, then another that we built ourselves to fulfill our most fervent need—to hit toward the chicken-wire outfield fence. I remember vividly the day I lofted my first home run over its distant uprightness, after which the field was moved again—it was too close to the parked cars, and we lost too many balls in the high weeds beyond the fence—moved to a site utterly remote from fences, and my days as a home-run hitter vanished abruptly and forever.

I learned to hit through the hole to right, coached by my father, who had played second base for a much-achieved Arbor Hill team ("The Little Potatoes, they're hard to peel"), at the turn of the century. He was a Yankee fan, as was Lou. I liked the Giants and the Red Sox. I gave my father a book on the Yankees, the only book I ever knew him to read all through; I later gave him one on the Red Sox but I don't think he even cracked it. He took me to Yankee Stadium and we saw Lou Gehrig hit what seemed to be a mile-high infield fly that turned out to be a home run over the right-field fence.

My father read newspapers, as we all did in the family, and his good pal was Charley Young, the sports editor of the *Knickerbocker Press.* We subscribed to the *Knick* and the *Times-Union* and the *Albany Evening News,* and frequently the *Daily News* and the *New York Mirror* turned up, all these papers bringing the writings of Dan Parker and Paul Gallico and Jimmy Powers and Damon Runyon into the living room; and so baseball became almost as pervasive and significant in my life as church and school.

School was inimical to life on opening day when the Albany Senators of the Class A Eastern League took to the field at Hawkins Stadium in Menands, just north of North Albany, our backyard, really. The stadium seated about eighty-five hundred, but eleven thousand would crowd in for special games. All season long we'd find a way to get in, either by shagging a foul ball that came over the wall, which got you in free when you returned it, or waiting for the friendly Menands village cop (Lou remembers he was overweight and his name was Thorpe) to hook us up with a ticket buyer ("Here's your son, Mister"), for if you arrived with a parent, then the boy scrambled under the turnstile, free. Bob Burns also recalls crawling under the fence near the bleachers. I don't remember doing this, and Joe Keefe says he lacked the bravery such crime required. Sometimes we actually paid to get in.

Joe remembered Como Catelli, a dramatic outfielder for the Senators who caught fly balls with dives, falls, tumbles, and other acrobatics, and Joe thought this was how it was done until he saw Joe DiMaggio let the fly balls drop quietly into his peach basket with that easeful DiMaggian ubiquity.

It is perhaps banal to remember Babe Ruth, but it is inevitable. Nobody went to school when he came to Hawkins Stadium, first on August 9, 1929 (I missed that one), and maybe five more times in the thirties, one of those nights memorable to us all because the Babe poked one into right-center that landed on the roof of the Norwalk burial vault company where spectators sat to watch the games free; and that was the longest ball anybody—Lou, Bob, me—ever saw hit in Hawkins, although the same was said of the Babe's center-field blast in '29. Hyperbole is always generational. The Babe himself said in Albany that the longest ball he ever hit was in Tampa, and it went about five hundred feet.

Richard J. Conners, the New York State Assemblyman from Albany, who was both the Senators' official scorer and local correspondent for the *Sporting News* from the early thirties to the postwar years, and a neighbor of mine for much of my life, tells me the Babe hit his last home run at Hawkins Stadium when he played an exhibition game as coach and first baseman for five innings (his knees were gone and he couldn't run) with Brooklyn, against the Senators, on July 25, 1938.

The attendance record that night, with all passes suspended, reached an all-time high: 11,724 fans cheered the Babe and saw him swack a curveball ("It broke like it was rolling off a table. I don't know how he ever hit it," said the catcher) over the right-field wall.

The Babe was expansive that night and said Albany was a "real good baseball city, one of the best minor-league cities in the country." He also reported that he was offered the job of managing Albany when it was in the International League, but friends warned him against taking it; and yet he might have accepted had the salary been right. But it wasn't.

When the Senators weren't at Hawkins, we followed them with great passion even so—hearing the away games announced on radio by, first, Doc Rand, then his son, Gren, who weren't away themselves, but reading the teletype in an Albany radio studio. They would vivify the wire news with sound effects, a snap of their fingers signifying a crack of the bat, their imagination supplying the "curveball that cut the outside corner," when all the wire offered was "strike two." We believed in the snap and the curve and were grateful for the fantasy.

We remember Pete Gray, who played with Elmira against Albany during the war, when most able-bodied players were in service, and in 1945 played a big-league season with the St. Louis Browns: an odd figure, a showpiece, really, but a triumph of willfulness over the adversity that had been his since his right arm's amputation in childhood.

We particularly remembered Ralph Kiner because, of all Albany Senators, he rose highest, becoming a major slugger for the Pirates (Albany was then a Pirate farm team, and so my National League allegiance was torn between New York and Pittsburgh) and a Hall of Famer (fifty-one home runs in 1947, fifty-four in '49, forty-seven in '50, and, in the '49 season, the first player in history to hit four home runs in four consecutive times at bat— twice.) He played left field for Albany in 1941 and 1942 and was a home-run hero even then. Bob Burns remembered the fans calling him "Wiggles" because when he gave three shakes of his tail it meant the next pitch stood a very good chance of going over the wall.

Baseball players were not only local heroes, they also, on occasions, turned into real people. They ate in the Morris Diner where we all hung out. Kiner roomed across from Bob Burns's house on Lawn Avenue. And Lou remembered seeing Jake Powell, an outfielder with the Yankees, at one of the late-thirties World Series games. When Jake saw Lou Pitnell, Sr., the North Albany barber who had cut his hair when he played with the Albany Senators, Jake gave him and his son a very big pregame hello, another reason for young Lou to be a Yankee fan forever.

Maybe the funkiest Albany saga is the story of Edwin C. (Alabama) Pitts, who was doing time in Sing Sing in 1935, for being the getaway driver in an armed robbery, when the Giants played a prison team as part of spring training, and somebody noticed Pitts had talent at the plate as well as at the wheel.

Dick Conners, who still lives in North Albany and was a friend of Pitts, told me the Pitts story.

The owner of the Senators in 1935 was Joseph Cambria, who put Albany into the International League, where it played from 1932 to 1936. Cambria, a noted figure in Baltimore laundry circles before entering baseball, heard about Pitts's talent, met him at the Sing Sing gate when he was paroled, and brought him to Albany. Albany's greatest local hero at that time was Johnny Evers, a Troy native but an Albanian by adoption, who had played big-league baseball for eighteen years, twelve of them with the Cubs; was the National League's Most Valuable Player in 1914; and was part of the great double-play combination that Franklin P. Adams had so deftly defined in the *New York Globe*:

... Trio of Bear Cubs fleeter than birds,
Tinker-to-Evers-to-Chance.
Ruthlessly pricking our gonfalon bubble,

Making a Giant hit into a double,
Words that are weighty with nothing but trouble.
Tinker-to-Evers-to-Chance.

After he left big-league baseball, Evers signed on with
Cambria as general manager of Albany, and in June of
1935 he inherited Alabama Pitts. Cries rose up against a
felon playing for the Senators, and William G. Bramham,
head of the minor leagues, ruled against Pitts.

Evers took the case to baseball's commissioner, Judge
Kenesaw M. Landis. Evers had already put himself
squarely behind Pitts. "I have been in baseball all my
life," he said. "If this boy is not allowed to play, I will
sever all connections with the game for good. That's a
broad statement, but I mean every word of it."

Landis ruled for Pitts, who came to Hawkins Stadium
to play outfield, and, as Ring Lardner once put it, although he was a mediocre fielder he was also a very poor
hitter. However, he was deft at cards, and Dick Conners
took him to play (across the street from my house) with
Dr. Jay McDonald and Jake Becker, among others; and on
the way home Pitts told Dick: "Don't stay in the game
when I raise a second time. I can read those cards."

Of course Dick imparted this news to the others and
that was that for Alabama's poker playing in North
Albany. But he concluded his days four years later with
another kind of gambling—knifed to death in Gastonia,
North Carolina, while dancing with another man's wife.

Pitts only lasted in Albany for six weeks, but the Senators went on for twenty-three more years, peaking in
1948 when attendance reached 210,804, or about 3,100 per
game—and standing-room only for Sunday doublehead-

ers. They went on to win the pennant in 1949. But a decade later professional baseball died in Albany, with attendance down to 40,000, and in 1960 the splendid Hawkins Stadium was razed, and sold to developers who put up a large cut-rate store called Topps. A friend of mine spoke for all baseball fans when she said, "Topps is the bottoms."

Baseball came back to Albany in 1983 when the Albany-Colonie Athletics, farm team of Oakland, was established in Heritage Park, near Albany Airport. In 1985 the team became the Yankees—a New York Yankees farm—and that year 324,003 people came to watch, an all-time seasonal attendance record for Eastern League baseball. I live on the other side of the river and since the games are no longer in my backyard, I follow them with great good will, but chiefly in the morning paper.

WHEN I LEFT North Albany for the first time I took a job at the *Glens Falls* (New York) *Post-Star* as a sportswriter. I covered all sports, wrote a column, and became a dogged fan of Red Smith, Joe Palmer, and Jimmy Cannon, who were heroic sportswriters of that age; and when I was drafted during the Korean War my time with sports served me well. The army made me a sports editor of a weekly newspaper, and so for the next two years I was so immersed in games that the rest of the world was minimalized.

This, of course, was temporary insanity, and at the end of my stint with the army I abandoned sports for the police beat, politics, and fiction, more expansive ways of indulging dementia. But sports, and especially baseball, lurked insidiously in my imagination and, when I began to write long fiction, the figures from childhood and sportswriting days demanded attention. Their stories seemed then, and now, elemental to my own life and the life of my family.

One of my great-uncles was Eddie (Coop) McDonald, a third baseman who was a maestro of the hidden-ball trick. He had three years (1911–13) with Boston and Chicago in the National League that were respectable but less than stellar, and another ten or more great years with minor-league teams in Birmingham, Chattanooga, and Little Rock as a player and manager. He was a beloved figure in the family, in my own memory, in Albany, and in the baseball world, and I drew on his experience, but not on his personal life, when I created Francis Phelan, the derelict hero of *Ironweed*. Francis was a drunk, Coop a teetotaler.

There is a quasi-mystical postscript to the *Ironweed*–Albany Senators connection. When the film was shot in Albany the old all-night Boulevard Cafeteria, one of my youthful haunts, empty in 1987, but its stained glass windows and murals still handsomely intact, was refurbished by the movie crew and used as the Gilded Cage, the saloon where Francis (Jack Nicholson) and his friend, Helen, go, and where Helen (Meryl Streep) sings so memorably. The Boulevard building was, and is, owned by Matt (Babe) Daskalakis, a first baseman for the Senators in the team's latter days in the mid-1950s. Since the movie, Matt has opened the place as a saloon, restaurant, and the only place in town where you can dance to the music of the 1930s and 1940s. Some things, clearly, were meant to be.

IF I HAVE come full circle from those games of catch and fungo in the mid-1930s to a latter-day faith in the annual ritual of baseball, it is not with any speculative or mythifying baggage, or any abstract rationale for what has come to pass, but rather it is with the still-visible specifics of memory: my uncle Peter swinging a bat and revealing to me what he looked like when he was fourteen; umpire Mike Pantone wearing a catcher's mask too small for his head, but protecting his nose; that rainmaker of a fly ball that Gehrig hit; that jazz language that came out of a Jimmy Cannon column.

These things accumulated and did what they did to me, and now here I am again, about to enter into my annual six months of daily anxiety over the fate of the New York Mets. I have good reasons for this, of course, as you now know.

The Psychic Hat

ANNE LAMOTT

My family's first home was a little coffee-colored house at the foot of a hill below a little white church. It is the house in which I became a Giants fan. It was old and small and funky, and it is no longer there. As it changed hands over the years, rooms and wings were added on, dazzling new gardens grew, and then the whole thing was torn down, and an infinitely grander and more streamlined house replaced it, something from *Architectural Digest*, and it must be worth close to a million dollars now. When we lived there, though, the kitchen was just barely big enough for the small table in its center, and I remember coming into the kitchen at three and four years old to find my mother and older brother sitting at this table, hunched over the radio, listening to a Giants game with such concentration that it might have been the first news reports from Pearl Harbor.

We were always Giants fans. It wasn't always easy over

the years because—and I mean this in the nicest possible way—they almost always screwed up somehow. You felt that they could have been in first place, with thirty games left to play, and could somehow have lost all thirty games. All through the years we worried that maybe, secretly, they were among the teams, like the Cubs and the Red Sox and the Indians, who seemed destined not to win it all. And that it was literally destiny, it was Sophocles, and there was nothing you or anyone else could do about it, any more than someone could flag down Oedipus and cry out to him, "No, no, Oed, don't kiss the girl, she is *trouble*." But rooting for the underdog is to root for oneself, and it is the stuff of noble tragedy—we're really better, but the bullies always win.

The Giants moved to San Francisco when I was four years old, and my mother, who was a wonderful athlete, fell in love with Willie Mays, even though a lot of fans gave him a hard time at first. Even my father, although he was not really a sports fan, liked to listen to the games on the radio. Sometimes at night friends of his and my mother's would stop by, and just for background music, like the auditory equivalent of a fire in the fireplace, the game would play softly from the kitchen; and I remember my older brother straining to hear the game from the bedroom we shared, straining in the dark. And when the voices of the grown-ups got too loud, I'd hear the small tramp of footsteps as he'd sneak to the door, whispering softly, pleading to himself for the adults to be more quiet so he could hear.

I don't remember exactly how old I was when my father took us to Candlestick for the first time, but I was little, and I think he must have been writing a story about it because he didn't like crowds or the parking hassles, and he normally took us to the zoo or the aquarium or to hang out in the sun with his other weirdo lefty writer friends. But we did end up at the 'Stick, and I remember holding his hand and being led down the aisle and, in my memory, my head was level with all those seats, and I remember being awestruck, absolutely blown away by the whole bright green overlit space. It was like seeing Oz. You walked up all those stairs and then stepped into the stadium, and this whole unreal world would be spread out before you, and you would step into it, into all that you had fantasized about as you listened to the radio—the incredibly beautiful grass field, and strangely reddish dirt, the gunfire of batting practice, and, oh, God, the players. When the game started, my daddy pointed out *Willie Mays*, for God's sake, and it was like finding Jesus out there in center field. And I got a golden glow in my stomach from all that energy.

I think we must have sat, that first time, close to the field, because everything seemed so incredibly vast, the outfield felt so huge that it was like discovering Greenland—you wondered, What will we do with all this land? How will we fill it? And you'd think it would take twenty people to cover it, instead of three; and there were so many thousands of people in the stands, a million times more people than you'd ever seen in one place before. And it was probably the first time you felt a cell membrane of belonging cover you and all these strangers, a cell membrane making you all one. You got to be a part of the pulse, the collective heartbeat, a beat so strong that you could feel it as you walked through the parking lot to the stadium: you got to be a part of a healthy mob.

I couldn't wait to get back to Candlestick, and I still

feel that way today, even though the night games there always were and always will be about as cold as you can get this side of cryogenics. At the end of a particularly bad night, it is sometimes hard to remember which population you belong to: the cryogenically frozen, or the run-of-the-mill loyal Giants fans.

You go there partly because some of the things the players do are simply impossible, and this makes it actual magic. But you also go there for something maybe even more important. I think that one of the things that happens is that, over the years, as you grow up and get more into real life, you realize that almost none of the truths and ideals you were learning about in school applied—notions of honesty and goodness and patience and fairness and morality and truth and beauty, and that excellence will be rewarded and that the bad people will be punished—you figure out that all these truths that were drummed into us every day turned out to be a lie, except in one place: sports. There they were, those ideals, out on the baseball field. And I found myself wanting, more and more, to close out the real-life world that felt so nuts and hypocritical, and to spend more time in this place where there were rules to the game, even if people rode them as hard as they could.

I loved it all—the sounds of the plays and the crowd, the catcalls, the vendors, the announcements on the P.A.; the smells of dirt and grass and food and sweat and fear; the players, the beauty and the power, the great pleasure of the winchlike tightening in my gut, and below, as the pressure mounted. Juan Marichal's impossibly high kick, his foot actually over his head, and McCovey, the best hitter I ever saw, with that awesome

ripping swing, sending those killer line drives into the
stands, and you knew they were going to dent someone
or something when they landed, and even Gaylord Perry
with his sneaky little spitballs, so mean and snarly and
sweaty, looking like he came right out of the red-dirt
country of Georgia. But year by year I paid through the
nose for my fanhood, because I was a girl fan.

For those of us who were socialized into being slavering
black-belt codependents, what this meant was that, while
the boys and men got to care so much about winning, I
and a lot of the girls and women just wanted everyone to
get a chance to play. This is humiliating to admit, but it
is true. We also loved the brilliance and glory and finesse,
the almost psychotic degree of hard work it takes to be a
player, the grace of a great hitter or the mercury swiftness
of a double play, but at the same time I obsessed about
the hurt feelings of the players at the bottom of the order,
and I wondered, Would it be too *goddamn* much skin off
of anyone's nose to let them hit second, or third, maybe
once in a blue moon? Huh? And what about the guy who
always has to play right field—why don't you just make
him wear a sandwich board out there that says, Crappiest
Player on the Team? Would it be the end of the world to
let him play shortstop every third or fourth game? I know
there are millions of girl fans out there who grew up with
as much appreciation of pure mastery and achievement
and superiority as the next boy, who understood that this
was war, patriotism without all the bloodshed, girls who
grew up to be women who read box scores over their
morning coffee with that stoned-out, shutdown, obsessive zombie look that men get while reading them,
where your hair could be on fire and they just hold up

their forefinger to indicate that they just need *one* more minute. But for a lot of us, it was Hemingway's question, of whether at a bullfight you identify with the bull or the bullfighter, and we identified with the bull, and we identified with the men who were eighth and ninth in the order, and with the forlorn guy out in right field.

I remember being at a game at Candlestick when I was twelve or so, and for some reason loving Tito Fuentes more than life itself, maybe partly because I loved to cry out his name with everyone else, "Teeeee-to, Teeeeee-to," it made me feel like someone from *West Side Story*, and something bad happened, he really screwed up big time and got booed, and I couldn't blink for the longest time, and had to hold onto my stomach and rock autistically to keep from crying. And I felt for the first time that if I could just talk to him, he'd want to be friends with me—he'd come to my house and we'd have a nice barbeque for him and my mother would beam a lot and he'd play catch with me and my brothers, and talk to my dad about books. After that I always had that feeling about baseball players, that they were regular guys, that they would want to be friends. Maybe it's because they were more like you—basketball players were too crazily tall and fast and football players were morbidly obese and grunty, but you sort of feel like you're made of the same basic stuff as baseball players. Baseball is so egalitarian— anyone, even a five-foot-two-inch pencil-necked geek can grow up to be a baseball great. (Anyone except a girl, of course. But this does not mean that as a girl, you can't get into the vicariousness of it all—you still get to live in the bodies of the players, and it lifts you out of your own fumbling body. And even if you're a girl you never stop believing that one day you'll throw out the first pitch on opening day, and the sold-out crowd will gasp and rise to its feet as one. A friend of mine, the great novelist Martin Cruz Smith, who's a good athlete and who had dreamed this very dream for forty-some years, actually got to pitch one pitch at Candlestick, and when I asked how it had gone, he said, "I looked like an old man doing the shot put for the first time.")

I went to a lot of games during my teens, with a bunch of kids who lived in Berkeley whose father was dead and who were allowed to drive even though they did not have driver's licenses, because their mother was Chinese and did not entirely understand the rules. The one who was fourteen was the best driver, but usually the fifteen-year-old boy would drive us to Candlestick—the A's had not yet moved to Oakland—and I really feel that it saved me, to belong to this ragtag little family, and also to get to wear, at Candlestick Park, that hat of belonging. You and thousands of other people are all wearing this psychic hat, this hat that proclaims, "We are this tribe. And I belong to it." But on top of it all we wore actual hats, Giants caps, black and orange, and they were, for me, along with the seriously bald, the great equalizer.

I had funny hair, crazy curly Albert Einstein dandelion patch hair, but at twelve or thirteen I discovered this fabulous green stuff in the stores that looked and felt like badly made Jell-O, but when dry made your hair feel like it had been shellacked, and it made your hair unmoveable—a typhoon couldn't have moved my hair; even the winds at Candlestick couldn't move my hair. And there at a baseball game, wearing my Giants cap, with just a few shellacked bangs poking out under the

brim, I fit in. It was a fabulous team—Mays and Mc-
Covey were still around, as were those nice Alou boys;
Orlando Cepeda had not yet been hurt, the crowds were
loyal, adoring; and *I fit in.*

Amped out of your mind on hormones and general
otherness, you got to sit there in a place where people
were doing things well—hitting home runs, stealing
bases, pitching shutouts—where you could lose yourself
and fall into this thing that was so much bigger, and you
got to get out of your body, out of your nutcase hair and
your weirdo parents and the whole death-dance that is
called junior high and high school and not quite disap-
pear, but rather *merge.* And you got to witness and be
part of this huge struggle, where people were winning
and losing and triumphing and being humiliated, and it
wasn't you: good God Almighty, for once it wasn't you.

(Speaking of Whom, I recently asked a priest friend
what he thought God would make of the game, and he
said that he thought God would have a problem with the
fact that someone has to win and someone has to lose,
because God is there to see that everyone wins. But that
still, if a man commits some horrible bonehead error, and
the whole game goes seemingly straight down the laundry chute, and the man goes from hero to goat, then the
miracle, the evidence of grace, is to watch the player in
the next game or even the very next inning end up
playing like a rebel angel, totally out of his head—steely-
eyed and sure. And as my priest friend says, God just
loves this sort of shit. But to tell you truth, I am more and
more convinced that God's real interest in baseball is
watching the hard-core born-again Christians come up to
bat and strike out.)

Part of what makes being a fan so enormously satisfying is that you get to hate all the other teams. When the A's moved here from Kansas City in my teens, it became tempting to defect—it's such a wonderful feeling to win, it has definitely got it all over the rewards of being loyal—but I didn't do it, not once. It would have been easy to root for the A's, just as, by the same token, it's easy to root for the 49ers, because you know they're going to be good, and so you get to relax about a lot of things. You know there's no way they'll have a terrible year; you know they won't disgrace themselves. So it's either very touching or sort of pathetic and doggy to be someone who, year after year, all season long, pulls so desperately for the Giants, who you're almost sure will end up having a bad year. I can't tell you how many times I have wanted to switch over. Some rabid Giants fans actually follow and care for the A's, but I am not that interested in this sort of person. That kind of thinking does not speak to me of a rich spiritual life and healthy boundaries. I love the city of Oakland, and I love the people, but I just don't like the A's. I know they're a great team. I just don't like them. They're a designer team. The whole scene feels too antiseptic—the stadium is so clean and perfect, as opposed to poor old Candlestick, where, on top of everything else, you've got that surrealistic veil of hot dog wrappers covering the entire field. It's like something you'd find on the set of an Italian opera, this shimmering, undulating veil of paper. It's hard to take your eyes off, and you kind of miss it when you go over to Oakland. And I don't like the A's uniforms: they're too clean and the colors are so bright and life-affirming in an obnoxious sort of way. I mean, green and yellow, for

God's sake—I know they are referred to as being green
and gold, but I've seen them—I'm not blind—and they're
lemony yellow, lemony yellow and green, like spring,
like a commercial for feminine sprays. Whereas the
Giants wear black and orange, mysterious and dark and
evil, and what with all that eye-black, it is like Ingmar
Bergman staging this year's Halloween pageant.

Plus, and this is really hitting below the belt, the
Oakland fans make me uncomfortable. A lot of them are
too antiseptic, too. You just can't shake the feeling at the
Coliseum that a lot of these people eat three square
meals a day, and no snacks, and are mostly not too
alcoholic, and when you're really feeling mean, you
think of them all as quiche-eaters. Over at the 'Stick,
however, about half the fans look like the cast from *One
Flew Over the Cuckoo's Nest*. They look like they
survive largely on fats, sugar, and carcinogens. I like that
in a people. They eat like I do, which is to say, poorly.
They do not, like the A's fans, eat oat bran and are not at
all careful about eating a certain number of vegetable
units a day, and they do not substitute yogurt for sour
cream on their baked potatoes. Maybe it's just that the
Giants were the first team I followed, or maybe it's, as
my younger brother suggests, like a sexual preference,
where by the time you're twelve, it's just gelled inside
you. But Giants fans are just so beautifully odd. The last
time I was at Candlestick was on one of those rare killer
balmy nights you get every so often where you're sitting
there, in what has become an old ballpark, watching
big-league baseball and feeling these waves of brotherly
love for Robby Thompson and Matt Williams, and that
everything's all right with the world; and there were

actually two nuns there that night, three seats over, and next to them this fabulous Boy George guy and over to my right was this man I'm convinced was Jeffrey Dahmer. ("Jeffrey, you're not eating.") Behind us all were five massively fat guys with beer bellies and no T-shirts, ashen and filthy as chimney sweeps, who had tried to spell out *GIANTS* by each writing a letter on their chests, but since there were only five of them, they spelled *GANTS*, and they were doing these five-man waves, and it was making us all laugh, including the nuns, and feel like we'd died and gone to heaven.

MY one real lapse as a fan was during my twenties. I didn't go to many games. I was living in Bolinas and it was too far a drive and I was feeling cynical about what I perceived as the loss of innocence in baseball, all those trillion-dollar salaries and all that dope and free agency, and brattiness, and doubleknit uniforms, and over in the American League, those rotten whores of Babylon, the designated hitters, who (I feel) besmirch us all—how are they any different than the guys who took Teddy Kennedy's exams for him at Harvard? But when I did go back finally, for a Saturday afternoon game, I fell in love all over again. God, I love the Giants, and hate whomever they're playing (even though I still secretly want everyone to get a chance to play). (And feel sorry for the guys batting eighth and ninth.) I felt once again how powerful this we/they psychology is, and that it's a wonderful feeling, intensely primitive—they are feelings we've always had, we have always felt good about us and bad about *them*, all the way back to our monkeyhood. And I

felt all over again that baseball not only gives us a
wonderful catharsis, it can actually give us back ourselves. We're a crowd animal, a highly gregarious and
communicative species, but the culture and the age have
put almost everyone into little boxes, all by ourselves—
yet baseball gives us back all of that stuff. It restores us.
And I also discovered, maybe most importantly, the
advent of tailgate parties.

Tailgate parties are one of the great inventions of
modern society. Everything is so crowded now, and there
are too many people and too many things to get done, and
consequently there are far too few opportunities to have
a feast. But I found people having actual feasts on the
tailgates of their trucks and the trunks of their cars, and
the people whom I was meeting had stopped just short of
an actual luau—there was everything but poi and an ice
swan centerpiece. I couldn't believe my eyes. And some
of the people in our party were friends of my friends, so I
didn't even know them, and there was something biblical
about the whole thing. It's the story of Ruth: you arrange
to meet a bunch of people at the stadium, and it turns out
that they have prepared a feast for you, and that these
people are your people, and where you go, they will go,
and their gods and heroes will be your gods and heroes,
and their food your food.

I've been going back ever since. Not just for the tailgate
parties, not just for those motion-picture moments that
only happen otherwise in the movies, but because, in
some nonsentimental way, baseball lets you be a kid
again, without being a fool. Everything is so green, and
it's spring and then summer, and everything speaks of
freshness and freedom. The first glimpse of the field each

time still gets me, like a beatific vision, makes me feel like the little kid in *Close Encounters of the Third Kind*, hits me with that sense of wide-openness, of feeling embraced in the circumference of the whole stadium. It lets me be a part of the struggle with winning and losing, and coming through at the last minute, and triumphing over adversity. I never, ever tire of watching the fans, and over and over watching great athletes handle massive failure with character and even (sometimes) dignity— even the best batters miss seven out of ten times. And it's about hope: it says there really isn't anything we can't do. It says that Dave Dravecky pitched again, and *won*, and it was sad when his arm broke a couple of months later, but even Lazarus had to die again, and it doesn't mean it wasn't a miracle. Life throbs with hope, or it wouldn't exist, and baseball throbs with hope, and greatness, and failure, and grace, and ridiculousness. Maybe in the old days, or at least in my memory, a great game felt as simple and clean as a Wendell Berry essay, but in spite of it all, in spite of the money madness and rages and drugs and whatever, in spite of it being something new and streamlined and hot, it is still also all that it ever was, slow and strange and funky as that coffee-colored house that is no longer there.

Surrogate Family

J. ANTHONY LUKAS

When I was four years old, my mother took me to my first evening at the theater—*The Bumblebee Prince*, an operetta by Rimsky-Korsakov, based on a story by Pushkin. By all reports, I was utterly entranced and, when the curtain came down, inconsolable.

"Oh, I'm so sad," I wailed. "I want to be back in that land. It's much nicer than this one."

It was a theme to which I returned frequently in my young life: the realm of fantasy versus the real world, a juxtaposition in which I invariably came down on the side of illusion.

On more than one occasion, according to notes my mother took in my "baby book," I was not altogether sure which was which. At age five, I asked at supper one night, "Is this fork real? Is this spoon real?" Uncomforted by my father's stern assurance that the tableware was quite substantial, I proclaimed: "I think this whole life is a dream—Mommy is a dream and Daddy is a dream and those candies are a dream. But if I asked for a candy and you wouldn't let me have it, I'd knock the whole dish down and it would make such a crash that everyone would wake up."

Not long thereafter, I announced the arrival of "Jova," an imaginary playmate who quickly became my faithful companion on auto trips, at mealtimes, and in bed. My mother speculated that he—I think it was a he—was a substitute for lost friends in a former play group, or perhaps an ally against my husky new brother. Whatever his provenance, Jova seemed as "real" as any other being in my universe.

This confusion of realms may have been partly explicable by our family's heavy psychic investment in the theater. My father's cousin was Paul Lukas, a matinée idol in his native Hungary who fluttered not a few hearts in this country as well, going on to win an Academy Award for his performance in Lillian Hellman's *Watch on the Rhine*. My mother also spent her young adulthood in the theater, studying at London's Royal Academy of Dramatic Art before touring for a time with Eva Le Gallienne. As soon as my younger brother and I could walk and talk, she directed us in miniature productions, earnestly rehearsed on the spacious window seats of our living room, then performed for many an unwary visitor. Much of our repertory was my own work, for I wrote eleven "plays" by the time I was eight—my favorite a wartime melodrama called "Prussia under Pressure."

But my preference for fantasy over fact may have been grounded less in theatrical make-believe than a child's intuition about the contrast between our family's appearance and its reality. By the late thirties, my father was

prospering as a Manhattan criminal lawyer. He and my
mother had purchased—and amply renovated—an 1820s
farmhouse set on six wooded acres in White Plains.
Bright flower beds rimmed the lawn, a rock garden graced
the adjacent hillside, and behind the house was a pond,
where on languorous summer afternoons my brother and
I rowed our dinghy and chased bullfrogs in the rushes.

But this air of bucolic contentment disguised crueller
truths. Beautiful and talented as she was, my mother was
a manic-depressive. Shortly after my birth, she tried to
kill herself. On several occasions, she was confined for
weeks to a mental hospital. Tortured by her illness and
by his own self-doubts, my father drank too much. And
he incubated the tuberculosis which emerged full-blown
in 1941 shortly after my mother succeeded in killing
herself.

Little wonder then that I retreated whenever possible
into that other world, where bumblebee princes soared to
the stars. I was in search of a realm which made more
sense than this one, a place in which beauty and virtue
and talent were rewarded not by pain and death, but by
the love and approbation they deserved.

It was then that I found baseball.

My first memories of the game are of listening to the
Yankees on a radio in a stuffy little room over the garage
occupied by a husky black man named Proctor Davis,
who served as the family chauffeur, gardener, and general
factotum. My father wasn't much of a ball fan (what
little enthusiasm he could muster fastened on the Pirates,
a residue of his childhood years in Pittsburgh). So it
remained for Proctor to initiate me in the mysteries of
the "paaastame," as he called it in his rich Georgia

accent. The first game I can remember hearing must have been in the summer of 1938—when I was barely five—for I recall that Lou Gehrig hit a prodigious home run that day, a clout reminiscent of his glory years, even though his production was tailing off by then, only months before he was diagnosed with the fatal muscle disease which would kill him three years later.

Though Gehrig was nearing the end, and Ruth, Lazzeri, Combs, Meusel, and Koenig were gone from the splendid teams of the late twenties and early thirties, the Yankees were still a powerhouse, capable of racing a little boy's heart: DiMaggio, Henrich, Dickey, and Gordon at the plate, Ruffing, Gomez, and Chandler on the mound. They won their third straight pennant that year, going on to flatten the Cubs in four games. In 1939, with Charlie "King Kong" Keller installed in right, they took still another pennant, winning an astonishing 106 games and finishing 17 games ahead of the second-place Red Sox; then they simply annihilated the Reds in the Series. For the first time in history, a team had won four consecutive pennants and four consecutive World Series. Again the anguished croak, "Break up the Yankees," was heard in the land.

To millions of Americans out there in the country's midsection, the Yanks were arrogant Olympians, big-city bullies who enjoyed beating up less-talented teams, bloated spoilsports who squeezed all innocent joy from the game. But to an anxious youth, still shaken by the implosion of his ordered world, the masterful Yanks were vastly reassuring. If I couldn't control my environment, they surely dominated theirs. And by some alchemy of fandom, their triumphs were mine as well.

I needed lots of reassurance. After my mother's death and the diagnosis of my father's illness, he went off for treatment at an Arizona sanitarium; our house was put up for sale, and my brother and I—aged seven and nine—were shipped off to a Vermont boarding school. That autumn, in the room we shared at Hickory Ridge, my brother, still a very small and frightened boy, cried himself into restless sleep night after night. I would surely have done the same had I not persuaded myself that nine year olds didn't weep.

In those first years at boarding school, as I fell prey to bouts of melancholy, the Yankees were one of the rocks on which I reassembled my life. All through the war years, I opened the paper each morning with a little shiver of anticipation, eager to see how "my" Yankees had manhandled the Browns or the Tigers. Seemingly invincible, they armed me for bruising encounters with a hostile world.

They did something more as well. Not surprisingly, what I missed most in those years was the very notion of family, the ingathering of Lukases each night in that comfortable old house, the sense that people I loved and who loved me were there at the close of each day no matter how I'd fared on the history quiz or how many goals I'd blown in soccer practice. With mother dead, dad in Arizona, the White Plains house now filled with strangers, our only "home" my maternal grandmother's New York apartment where we spent vacations from school, it was hard to believe in an entity called the Lukases.

Before long the Yankees became my surrogate family. It was a curious, makeshift clan during the war: thickening journeymen named Etten, Metheny, Stirnweiss, Johnson, and Grimes. But I tracked their exploits across the sports pages as intently as ever I did the advance of Patton's tanks on the *Times*'s war maps. I knew where Nick Etten was born, how many years Bud Metheny had spent in the minors, what Snuffy Stirnweiss ate for breakfast, what size bat Oscar Grimes used, how Billy Johnson cared for his glove. Here were twenty-five versions of "Jova," the imaginary companion of my early childhood, keeping me company well into adolescence.

And there was always one special Yankee who spoke to me as no one else did. Through most of the forties, that was a long, lean outfielder named Johnny Lindell, who hit for average and power, and had an uncanny penchant for the timely hit. There was something in the very name *Lindell*—redolent of pickup games on new-mown Appalachian pastures—that captured for me the essence of this very American game. "Come on, Lindell," I'd chant to the radio, sequestered under my pillow on sticky summer nights, "Come on, Johnny, hit one for me!"

Yet, in those boyhood years, baseball remained largely an abstraction for me. It will surprise no one to learn that on real dirt and sod I was, at best, an indifferent ballplayer. For some reason, very early on, I opted for third base, though the wicked grounders and angry line drives which scorched down that line held special terrors for me. All through the elementary grades and into high school, I'd stand there as balls ricocheted off my chest and arms, scrambling to retrieve them in time for a desperate heave to first. But I don't recall getting many runners out. And I never hit worth a lick. After a single year as a seldom-used reserve on the high-school team, I heeded the manager's blunt suggestion that I take up tennis.

Moreover, for one whose fantasy life was so engaged with baseball, I saw surprisingly few games firsthand during those years. After my father returned healthy from Arizona, he'd occasionally take us out to Yankee Stadium (where, tongue firmly in cheek, he'd root loudly for the Pirates). I particularly relished that tingling moment, as one came off the Stadium ramp onto the first level, when the vivid green of the field leapt up at you with a sensuous rush. For me, in those years at least, the ballpark was less an athletic than an aesthetic experience. Those dazzling pinstripes against all that green never failed to take my breath away.

But somehow the game's mystery was less compelling at the Stadium than it was alone in my room at night, the radio tuned to Mel Allen as he chanted the action in his liquid Alabama drawl.

Baseball and radio, it seemed to me, were blissfully compatible. The only major team sport which does not race against the clock, baseball's dreamy pace was perfectly suited to the rambling style of old-time radio. Moreover, radio fed the listener's fantasy, and baseball is a game that thrives on fantasy. Baseball broadcasting was often an art form because it left space for the listener to fill with his own secret musings (whereas television, always explicit and literal, filled the event entirely, squeezing out the intimations which could give it another dimension). For those of us who became fans in the forties and fifties the radio announcer was a potent figure: a secret companion for our loneliest hours; an uncle figure with whom to take our ease; an intriguing raconteur who spiced his tales with the lilting lingo of a more exotic world; a play-by-play man for our fantasies.

For more than a decade, Mel Allen played all those roles for me. As a student at Putney, the upper school of Hickory Ridge, I walked a couple of miles each day from the main campus down to the school theater, where my extracurricular life was centered. As I trudged across the cow-pocked pastures, my mind played endless interior games of baseball. One phrase in particular resounded on those walks—always, of course, in Mel Allen's meliflu-ous tones—"It's a hard ground ball down the third-base line, Lukas up with it on one hop, throws to second for one, over to first. A double play!" For years, when things weren't going quite my way, I'd play that line back in my head and, abruptly, I'd feel better.

Those were the years when the fierce Yankees–Red Sox rivalry reached exquisite consummation. Whenever the Red Sox and Yankees played head-to-head, the school's aficionados—among them, Chris Lehmann-Haupt, now the *New York Times* chief book critic—would creep down to the carpentry shop where we knew an old radio could be tuned to a Pittsfield station which carried the Sox. To this day, as I recall the autumn of '49, when DiMaggio and Williams led their mates to a deli-cious showdown on the final day, my nose sniffs the pine tar and wood shavings in that cluttered shop.

The addiction to baseball on radio has lasted a lifetime. In later years, wherever I was during the season, I'd flick on the radio to see if I could get a game, any game. I even fancy that I write better with a game on across the room, for it seems to me that baseball and writing enjoy a special affinity. Unlike any other sport I know, baseball is a linear game, falling naturally, play by play, inning by inning, into a story, an epic tale waiting to be told by men and boys in schoolyards or locker rooms, or late at night around beer-heavy tables.

As I grew older, the real-life story grew a bit soiled around the edges. The Steinbrenner years cured me forever of my Yankees addiction. For a time, while working on a book in Boston, I transferred my loyalties to the Red Sox, ancient rivals of my youth, whom I now elevated to a special rank of baseball purists, still playing on grass, in a park of human dimensions, before rabid, old-time fans. One year, I went to spring training in Winter Haven where I chronicled for the *Times* the emergence of a rookie Red Sox catcher named Gary "Muggsy" Allenson, who fitted my notion of what a gritty, knuckles-in-the-dirt ballplayer should be. Though Winter Haven was known then principally for huge black flies, remnants of the Ku Klux Klan, and the off-key trio at the Ramada Inn cocktail lounge, I attained a kind of baseball nirvana that spring.

But successive September debacles combined with the obtuseness of Fenway management pushed me ever deeper into the world of illusion. In 1981, I became a charter member of the nation's second Rotisserie league, my loyalties henceforth reserved for the "Palukas" (what else?). Now on soft summer evenings at the stub end of Long Island, I haunt the late-night sports roundups, desperate to know how Ruben Sierra, Ken Griffey, Rafael Palmeiro, Jim Abbott, and all the other Palukas are doing.

What can I say? Baseball reaches something deep inside me, stirring the guttering embers of memory and feeling. It keeps me in touch with the time when it was far more than a game or a pastime, but a buttress to my self-esteem, a substitute family, a cooling balm for my pain, a secret pleasure to my ear, a goad to my richest fantasies.

A Love of Fungo

GEORGE PLIMPTON

I suspect the fungo bat has as much to do with my love for baseball as anything else. I have scoured around for something with more universal appeal—so I can compare notes with other fans—but the bat is what continually returns to mind. For those unacquainted with the fungo bat (or its allure), it is, of course, the very long light bat used invariably by a coach in pregame practice—tossing the ball up with one hand and using the bat to hit grounders to the infielders, or high lazy flies to the outfield. The latter is what I prefer: the ball seems to spring off the bat swung with such nonchalant ease, and it rises until, golf ball–size, it hangs above the distant outfielders. And then I know nothing more satisfactory than hitting fungoes unless it's setting off fireworks: the same manifestations are involved—the upward rush of a projectile towards the sky . . . in one case propelled by the machinery of the body, in the other by the dip of a lighted flare to the fuse. Golfers, too, know something of this—the pleasure of defying gravity with the lofted shot, the ball poised at its apex over the distant green.

When I was a boy I loved hitting fungoes. Among other things it was far easier to do—toss a ball up and hit it—than standing in the batter's box and trying to connect with a pitch whipping in from the pitcher's mound. Nor was one the focus of the kind of attention one received up at bat—the kids jeering, calling in from their infield positions, or from the visitors' bench, only too presciently, "No hit! No hit!"

One preteen summer I invented a game of fungo-solitaire out behind the garage, which involved hitting stones into the woods. The other day I discovered the bat with which I did this—not a real fungo bat, of course, but an ancient lightweight Louisville Slugger, battleworn and badly chipped and nicked by the hundred of stones it had hit out amongst the tree trunks. The idea of the game was that if the stone, well hit, with a lot of loft, soared through the branches and popped a tree far back in the forest, it was a home run. Line drives that flicked through the leaves for a substantial distance were doubles, triples. Shots that sang along the ground were outs, as were line drives that hit the nearest trees. Sometimes the closest trees made splendid fielding plays! My lips moved briskly as I broadcast what was going on. Entire games were played—my beloved New York Giants, usually against the despised St. Louis Cardinals. I remember that it was Dick Bartell, the Giants' shortstop, who hit a foul ball that buzzed like a hornet into the side of the garage, missing a pane-glass window by an inch or so.

I have no idea what my parents thought of this. I was out there almost every day. The driveway showed patches where I had stripped away the stones and pebbles. One afternoon, unbeknownst to me, my father took a photograph from an upstairs window; the developed print was pasted in the family photograph album with the notation, "George at batting practice." I suspect my father assumed there was a practical reason for hitting stones into a forest . . . that perhaps I was sharpening my hand-eye coordination for the real thing. How could he have known that a World Series was going on out there and that Charlie "King Kong" Keller of the Yankees (alas! alas!) had just poled a long one off the Giants' Cliff Melton.

Ultimately I graduated from hitting stones to fungoing true baseballs to teammates during the various stages of my education; more recently, I have been hitting flies to my young son and his school friends. They stand at the end of the lawn, just at the edge of the potato fields. When we started this, years back, it scared them sometimes when I caught the ball just right on the bat and it swept up to an enormous height above them; under it the boys circled awkwardly, their stick-thin arms aloft, the fingers of their gloves spread wide, something prayerful about their attitudes, as if beseeching the ball to end up harmlessly in the pocket of a glove. Now they are far more nonchalant. If I can loft one into the potato fields, they step back among the furrows, head down to pick their footing, and then at the last, look up, pat the glove once, and catch the ball waist-level, à la Willie Mays.

We stay out there until the shadows are deep across the lawn or my hands begin to blister. A strange passion. And a pervasive one as well. To this day I enjoy getting to a major league ballpark early so I can watch the professionals do it—standing in the bare circular patch just off home plate and poling out high arching shots that rarely resemble the trajectories of fly balls hit in the game later on. I watch the clutch of outfielders out by the fence, seemingly disassociated from what the coach has just done, and then one of them, whose turn it apparently is, takes three or four languid steps and gathers it in, the ball dropping almost vertically into his glove. There is a quaint description of gathering in an easy fly ball from the nineteenth century that I relish. It comes from the sports pages of the *New York World*, October 26, 1889: "Ward's fungo was simply pousse-café for Corkhill, and he swallowed it smoothly."

Oddly, I have never actually used a real fungo bat. I picked one up one day in 1980 at spring training in Fort Lauderdale when I was getting ready to be the manager-for-a-day or so of the New York Yankees—a participatory journalistic stint that didn't work out because my chance of managing a game was cut short by the baseball strike that spring. It was called on the day of the game I was scheduled to manage—between the Yankees and the New York Mets. The day before, during practice, I saw the fungo bat leaning up against the bat rack, long and slender, and I gazed at it as if it were a witch's wand. Because of my position as the Yankee manager *pro tem* I considered walking out to one of the fungo circles with it and lifting out a few fly balls to the players lounging out by the fence. But never having used one before (it seemed far too slender to make easy contact) perhaps I would toss the ball up and miss it completely, or tap it down onto my shoes. Once again, like echoes from the past, the fielders would jeer in, "No hit! No Hit!"

So I resisted. But I picked it up to heft it just briefly, marveling at the lightness of it, and the feel.

There is a machine now which performs this lovely act—a fungo "bazooka," it's called—which propels baseballs out to the fielders with a kind of metallic *thunk*. It looks not unlike the machines wheeled out on airport tarmacs to start jet engines. I am a purist in these matters and would banish such machines from baseball. First of all, the bazooka has a military connotation which does not suit the pastoral nature of the game. And secondly, it is unthinkable aesthetically to have a snout-nosed machine, trailing a long electric cord, wheeled out to the fungo circle to perform this time-honored function. Admittedly, the coach who hits fungoes is hardly an aesthetic triumph—invariably grizzled, portly, too advanced in years to wear a baseball uniform with style—but this is tempered by the magical thing he does with the bat. In sum, he is an institution which should be declared off limits to machine-age dabblers, especially cost-actuaries who assure management that such devices are money-savers. I have been able to come to terms with the pitching machine—known as Iron Mike to the trade—because it saves wear and tear on the delicate instrument that is a pitcher's arm. But I cannot imagine what part of the human anatomy is damaged by hitting fungoes; surely the bazooka diminishes some portion of the human spirit that thrives on ritual and tradition.

My obsession with everything about the fungo prompted me some years ago to look into the derivation of the word itself. It turns out that no one is quite sure. William Safire once brought up the question of the etymology of *fungo* in his *New York Times* language column and got a lot of different replies from people professing to know. Among these were (1) that it derives from cricket where, if practice strokes were taken before the match, these were referred to as "fun goes" as in "I think I'll have a fun go"; (2) from a street game in which catching three fungoed flies qualified a player to trot in and take over the bat. The fielders would keep count: "one goes," "two goes," and then "fun goes" when the third catch was made; (3) that a fungo bat is so light that it can be compared to fungus; (4) that it comes from the word *fungible*, meaning something substituted, as in the thin fungo stick used instead of the conventional bat; (5) from the German *fangen* meaning to catch, suggesting that the emphasis of the early fungo games was catching rather than hitting the ball; (6) from a Scottish verb, *fung*, which means to toss, fling, pitch, along with the O ending so often used in games—beano, bingo, keno.

There were others, equally plausible or implausible. My desk dictionary says simply that the origin of the word is "unknown," just that, "unknown," like the soldier, and I suspect I prefer it that way. It somehow suits the essential character of those boyhood summer evenings . . . fungoing stones into the forest, lips moving busily to describe those titanic games . . . forgotten now, unknown, lost forever to memory.

Baseball Memories

STEPHANIE SALTER

As mementos go, it is an odd one. Even for baseball. Yet the mere thought of it packs all the nostalgic punch of a first pressed corsage or a cracked and faded photograph.

"It" is a standard leather lace from a pair of old deck shoes I used to wear when I was a sportswriter covering the Billy Martin–managed Oakland A's. The lace looks like any other leather thong except for one end, which is slightly melted and singed black.

The lace is scorched because two of the A's players, Steve McCatty and Mitchell Page, secretly attempted to set it on fire during a postgame interview in the clubhouse. This hopelessly juvenile practice, called *giving a hot foot*, was very big among the Athletics at that time. They did it constantly to other sportswriters, to TV guys, and, of course, to one another. It is typical of baseball, a perverse act of endearment that says, "We care."

When the players gave me a hot foot—or tried, because

leather does not combust as readily as cotton—I knew my relationship with the game had, at last, been consummated. I loved baseball; baseball loved me.

It is not my fault that I had to wait until I was well into my twenties to be born as a baseball fan. I grew up female in Indiana in the 1950s. Girls in general did not play baseball or any other team sport in that era. Midwestern girls in particular didn't even watch baseball because it was against our religion, which was high-school basketball.

From my hometown of Terre Haute, the nearest major league team was a four-hour drive north, south, or west, to Chicago, Cincinnati, or St. Louis. My small high school, which managed to produce three Olympic medalists, had a baseball team but nobody would have been caught dead going to a game. The uniforms were dorky, you know.

Baseball from this skewed perspective was Out There Somewhere. You could hear it happening on freak summer nights when the AM radio waves went awry and a Cards or Cubs game would crackle in over KMOX or WGN. (We never got the White Sox that far south—WMAQ didn't have the power—and the Reds might as well have been in Cuba for all the attention anybody in Terre Haute paid them.)

Alas, I remember almost nothing about this period—my baseball infancy?—but I would bet anything that although I didn't understand what they meant, my first words must have been *Ernie Banks*.

I did get intimately involved with the 1960 World Series but not for any of the right reasons. A boy on whom I had a terrific crush, Mike Turner, was a ferocious

Yankees fan. He believed he *was* Mickey Mantle. Naturally, because Mike Turner adored the Yankees and I adored Mike Turner, it was incumbent upon me to belittle his team and put my money where my mouth was. I became an overnight Pirates fan, and, to my shock and Mike Turner's horror, was rewarded when Bill Mazeroski homered in the ninth inning of the final game to ruin the Yankees' season and Mike Turner's young life.

In the interest of candor, I must tell you that I had to look up every fact in that last paragraph except Mike Turner's name and that the Pirates won the Series. I'm sorry. This is typical of my relationship to baseball—big screen, low resolution of detail—and I know that it drives most men crazy. In an ironic departure from traditional gender behavior, baseball turns men into detail freaks. (We women, after all, are supposed to be the sticklers for such minutiae as anniversary dates, fork placement, and the implied specificity of "I'll call you sometime this week," which means "by Wednesday.") For males, baseball detail is sacred blood; it continually fuels their passion for the game.

Personally, I view details as the reason God invented *The Baseball Encyclopedia* and nine thousand other compendia that are published each year by everyone from the *Sporting News* to junior college English professors. If you really must know which second baseman holds the record for Most Errorless Chances Accepted, Consecutive Seasons, you can find it in a book.

Didn't Casey Stengel say, "You could look it up"? Well, you can. I do. The game is still a joy to behold.

Gender is not the only factor that contributes to my benign neglect of baseball detail. When I first began covering baseball for a living (the beginning of a real relationship), I was the backup, backup baseball writer for the *San Francisco Examiner*. My task was to spell the two regular beat writers by covering whichever Bay Area team was the worst. As this was the mid-1970s, the final discount shopping days of Charles O. Finley and the last decade of the Giants' long pennant famine, I stayed busy.

More often than not, the teams I covered were, for all practical purposes, out of pennant contention by the All-Star break. The significant details—wins, batting championships, league-leading ERAs—were denied them and were of little use to me as their chronicler. So I concentrated on the big picture, the game of baseball itself, and on inconsequential details such as Billy North's penchant for dropping foul balls or Bob Knepper's coltish trot to the mound.

Instead of numbers, I paid attention to eel-like slides into second base, sloppy but effective bunts, or the heartbreaking way a big, overgrown man-boy's shoulders could sag when a 3-and-2 fastball down the middle screamed by and three men were left stranded.

Instead of feeling deprived, I consider myself special for having come at the game this way, late and through the back door. No offense, but men who grew up dreaming of being Joe DiMaggio or Don Drysdale or Willie Stargell are a dime a dozen. Lord knows sportswriting is not about to run out of them. Everybody and his Uncle Dick fell under baseball's spell when he was seven. Not me. I came to baseball a vote-casting, beer-drinking, deflowered, big-picture adult.

Baseball is the one game that can stand up to this sort of dual challenge, the one game that can seduce an adult woman as effectively as it can a seven-year-old boy. And, I firmly believe, it is a better game for the diversity of its fans. Baseball is very catholic (with a lowercase *c*), and its oft-trumpeted affordability compared to football or basketball must never bc taken lightly. Baseball's immortality lies in the fact that you can get everything you need and want out of the game without having to be a rich guy. And I do mean guy.

I did not set foot into a major league baseball park until I was twenty-two years old and already launched upon my first career as a fact-checker at *Sports Illustrated* magazine. It was a night game at Shea Stadium. I forget who the Mets were playing; it truly doesn't matter. What does matter and what I remember as if indeed it were yesterday was how fantastically, gorgeously, otherworldly green the field was under the night lights. It was one of the most beautiful things I had ever seen. Mesmerized and frozen in the aisle, I had to be shoved, literally, out of the way, something for which no one ever must wait long in New York City.

The only other clear memory I have of that night is the delight I felt at hearing the fans around me in the left-field stands rag unmercifully on Cleon Jones. I had nothing whatsoever against Cleon, which was more than most of his teammates could say. The product of a hyperpolite upbringing, I simply was thrilled to hear grown men and women call another grownup person a dog.

At this point I should address the probability that more than a few readers are irritated with me. What, they want to know, was a woman who had never been to a major league baseball game doing at *Sports Illustrated?* How, they snarl through gritted teeth, did she then land a job covering the Giants and A's for a daily newspaper?

Well, I did know how to keep proper score, if that is any help. Along with junior-high-school Latin and being able to drive a manual transmission car, I consider the ability to keep proper score for a baseball game among the top three skills that have made me what I am today. The simplest explanation, however, is that all of this happened during the 1970s, a time, you may recall, in which the civilized Western world and most of its values were turned upside down. The seventies set the stage for Ronald Reagan, remember? At the *Examiner*, for example, I was hired in 1976 by a man who had been given the job of sports editor precisely because he hated sports and knew even less about them than I did. This sort of thing happened all the time in the seventies.

And what of it? No one died because I covered baseball without ever having been spiked by a man sliding home. More significant, no one canceled a subscription to the *Examiner* because they felt cheated out of solid coverage. In fact, I won awards, developed a following, and became, more often than not, an outlet for many of the more personal and profound stories from the players because I was a woman and less threatening to a young man's fragile ego.

"But she hasn't played the game," I used to hear as often as I heard "The Star-Spangled Banner" in those days. "How can she write about it?"

Men and women who have never held public office write about the president and Congress every day. People who couldn't hit a high C if they had a gun held to their heads get paid to assess the performance of Luciano

Pavarotti. As I tell students in the journalism classes I am asked to address, a good reporter can cover anything, from nuclear physics to a stand-up double. The secret is to do your homework when there's time, ask lots of questions of the experts, and listen, really listen, to the people about whom you are writing.

Sometimes with a twenty-two-year-old infielder this is a Herculean task, but listen you must.

As for the more cosmic explanation of why I was afforded the privilege of entering into a relationship with baseball through the rarefied passageway of sportswriting, I like to think it was ordained by the Baseball Gods. You see, I was meant to love the game and to spread the word far and wide—I still find baseball the cleanest, most succinct metaphor for life's tests and rewards—but, starting so late, I had a lot of ground to make up in a short time.

I had to get as close-up and personal with baseball as you can without actually donning doubleknits and a protective cup.

Through baseball I learned nothing less than to like men. A lifelong heterosexual from a functional family, I had always loved men, found them attractive, and enjoyed their attentions to me. But I had no brothers or bosom boy pals during my childhood, so I did not know much about males, especially the why of their behavior. (If I had, I would have known better than to bet the Pirates against Mike Turner's beloved Yankees.) By the time I ran smack into the women's liberation movement in college, I saw precious few reasons to *like* men even if I couldn't live without them.

What baseball gave me at an advanced age, what it revealed to me as I watched and wrote about it day after day, was the excitement, beauty, and—God, I can't believe I'm saying this—the visible proof of an inherent sweetness in males at play. This was a huge missing piece of the puzzle for, as I now realize, if you don't know men at play, you don't know men. Watching *Bull Durham* helps, but it isn't the real thing. In the same vein, so too was I ignorant of the timeless nobility of a team. (Thanks to the women's movement and Title IX, young women of today do not know this deprivation.) I had observed teams from the sidelines as a cheerleader but I had never been inside the guts of one. To travel with two dozen men, to watch them put aside their wildly diverse personalities and sensibilities, subjugate themselves to the authority of one man, the manager, and unite in a common goal was impressive. Especially when I recall some of the managers Charlie Finley hired back in the late seventies.

Seeing these men sweat and stretch and run and crash into walls in pursuit of an activity they so obviously loved was poignant. Yes, despite all their carping about money and their petty, internal feuds, I believe that professional baseball players do love what they do and the majority would keep their same jobs even if the salaries were reduced to mortal proportions.

Admittedly, this love is difficult to detect during regular-season play. During championships something else kicks in that I believe is closer to war than love. But in spring training, baseball love is in bloom, which, no doubt, explains why spring training habitually brings out the poet—be it Keats or Kilmer—in every sportswriter. Spring training is baseball love on parade and, as others have written, it is a puppy love.

Spring training is what's left of the Way It Was.

Small(er) stadiums, old men in the stands hawking beers from ice-filled buckets, newly mown grass whose fragrance is a guaranteed nostalgia binge for any city-dweller. Crowds don't roar in spring training. Van Halen doesn't accompany a giant-screen instant replay on the scoreboard. People rarely bring Watchmans to the ballpark and fights almost never break out in the bleachers.

In spring training, fans get to hear the gen-u-ine "thwack" of a hardball hitting a catcher's mitt, they are privy to Monica Seles–like little grunts as their heroes leg out weak singles or dive for strong ones. The bat cracks louder. The grass stains brighter.

The players, too, are better in spring training because they are more human and thus easier to identify with. The pitcher is not a machine that hums along through seven innings until some microscopic chip wears out and he walks two and muffs a soft comebacker for E-1 and bases loaded. His physical effort is obvious, his tension real. The pitcher is responsible for keeping the lid on the whole works out there and all you have to do is look at him sweat to know that.

In spring training baseball is the way I like it best, languorous and dreamy with intermittent moments of precision and frenzy. The outcome, not to mention the score or who hit what directly to whom in which inning, is of no consequence. All that matters and the primary focus of everyone is the playing of the game. MEN AT PLAY.

When men play, time stands still for them and the people who watch them. I know this is one reason so many old people like baseball. It is not only their link to the past, it is one of the few activities in which they can engage that does not feel speeded up the way most of life seems to get as we grow older.

You see, as I mentioned earlier, I find baseball the most useful metaphor I have ever encountered. Although I have not covered the game for a living in more than a decade, my writing and speech still are peppered with baseball analogies. Baseball still helps me understand and explain Life Itself.

Batting slumps and hitting streaks, for instance, are splendid ways to illustrate some of the major truths of life. They are an affirmation that this, too, shall pass. They are evidence that Buddha was dead-on when he advised that the best way to find something is to stop looking so hard for it. And they are stellar examples that some things in this life simply can't be explained.

I mean, here you have a person hitting .388 in late May and then, in mid-August, here is the very same person hitting .190 *for no good reason.* Life is like that: things happen *for no good reason,* and the people who seem to make the best of it are the ones who know that, more times than not, you are better off waiting out the .188 than you are to start messing with where you put your back leg.

Lest I mislead with this emphasis on Zen and time and the beauty of men at play, baseball's nitty-gritty is not completely wasted on me. I no longer make my living in press boxes, keeping tabs on game-winning RBIs and men LOB. But when I am asked to name the most memorable sporting event I ever witnessed (and I am asked this more often than you might imagine), I never hesitate.

"I was in the park for one of Nolan Ryan's no-hitters," I always say. "It was the most exciting thing I ever saw in sports." And it was.

I had a great seat, not in the press box but in the lower stands along the first-base line. By the seventh inning, the entire crowd had begun to throb, just ever so slightly, with the possibility. Throughout Ryan's time on the mound in the eighth, everyone stood and followed each pitch as if it were carrying a load of nitroglycerine. By the ninth, the noise was continuous, rising from a mere din to a tempest's roar each time Nolie rared back and let fly.

I know it isn't possible—we were making too much noise—but it seems as though neither I nor anyone else breathed during the last three at-bats. We were all suspended there, tens of thousands of us, hanging over the stadium in a fragile and invisible net that threatened to break at any second but just couldn't, oh please, oh please, oh please, don't let it break.

And it didn't. Or maybe it did because something surely broke among us when the last man went down. But the break didn't hurt. It was exhilarating, a gigantic release. It was a big, fat collective orgasm, that's what it was, something a kid might *feel* but only an adult with some experience and sense of context could understand and identify.

So, did you notice that in that description I did not mention where the game was, on what date it was played, against whom, which of Nolan Ryan's seven no-hitters it was, or who the last batter happened to be and whether he struck out swinging or looking or flied out?

Does it make the story any more exciting to know that the game was played on June 1, 1975, in Anaheim against the Orioles? That it was the fourth of Ryan's seven no-hitters and it tied him then with Sandy Koufax for career no-hitters? That Dave Chalk scored the Angels' only run, that Ryan fanned nine batters, walked four, and that it was his fourth no-hitter in his last 109 starts?

OK. That last part is pretty interesting, I'll grant you. Four no-hitters in a little more than two years. But it's still an exciting story without that fact, and I was there and I remember. I saw the *game*. I looked up the details for you.

It's like my singed shoelace. To someone else it might seem incomplete, just a piece of scorched leather. To me it is metaphor, big picture, men at play, Life Itself. It is baseball, and it makes me feel good.

A Fan Reborn

ROBERT WHITING

You can credit the former clerk of Humboldt County, California, for initiating me to major league baseball. His name was Fred Moore, a big gregarious ex–redwood logger who, in the fall of 1954, owned one of the very few television sets in Eureka, a fog-shrouded port town on the northern coast of California which served as the Humboldt County seat. Fred was an old family friend, and he invited my father, a local businessman, and me to his house one Saturday morning to watch the fourth game of the 1954 World Series between the New York Giants and the Cleveland Indians. Until that day, I'd never seen a real baseball game—professional, amateur, or otherwise. I was vaguely aware of a semipro team in Eureka—the Humboldt Crabs—yet the only exposure that I, an eleven-year-old sixth grader, had previously had to the sport was in schoolyard softball workups.

My father, for his part, thought that football was the only game on God's earth worth watching. Still, the

prospect of seeing this wondrous new thing called television, which had only recently been made available to
our isolated community, years behind the rest of the
country, was enough to attract his attention, even if it
did mean having to watch baseball. Arriving at Fred's
front door, my father and I were ushered into the living
room, where Fred introduced us to his pride and joy—a
brand-new Philco box set, positioned on a table in front
of the sofa as if it were a family shrine. We were
immediately transfixed by the fuzzy, strangely elongated
images before us. The closeup shots of the dugout, the
view of Cleveland's Municipal Stadium, even the Gil-
lette "Look Sharp, Feel Sharp" commercials left us awestruck. Fred, already an accomplished TV viewer, was a
hopeless baseball addict, and he tried hard to focus our
minds on the game itself.

The Cleveland Indians, he explained, were the greatest
team in the entire history of baseball. They had three
twenty-game winners—Bob Lemon, Early Wynn, and
Mike Garcia—and that was about as good as you could
get, he told us. And what's more, they had Bob Feller,
who, in his prime, Fred declared, had been the most
phenomenal fastball pitcher known to man. Feller had
won thirteen games that season and was in the "twilight
of his career," according to Fred. But his presence in the
World Series was reason enough for any sane man to go
out and buy a TV—which was exactly what Fred had
done a week earlier.

Unfortunately, things were not going quite according
to Fred's plans. The New York Giants had a center fielder
named Willie Mays who, Fred grudgingly advised us, had
the talent of three ballplayers. In Game One, Mays had

made a miraculous over-the-shoulder catch while racing toward the outfield wall to steal certain victory from the Indians. The Giants also had someone named Dusty Rhodes sitting on the bench who, Fred suggested, was the luckiest pinch-hitter alive. Rhodes had come on to hit a game-winning home run after Mays's miracle catch, causing a thoroughly disgusted Lemon to throw his new-bought twenty-dollar glove into the stands and Fred to have an apoplectic fit. Fred still hadn't got over it.

"Goddamn Rhodes," he had bellowed, cursing New York's good fortune. "Probably closed his eyes when he swung."

The Giants had gone on to win the next two games, which only intensified Fred's anguish. Now it was do-or-die for his team, and Lemon started again, not Feller, as Fred had expected. Feller, in fact, had yet to make an appearance in the Series.

"What the hell's the matter with you guys?" he shouted at the TV. "Where in God's name is Feller?"

As the Giants knocked out Lemon and a succession of Indian relievers, none of whom was Feller, Fred grew more and more agitated. He had never seen Feller pitch, he told us, not even in movie newsreels, and this might be his last chance.What if Feller retired after the Series, as Fred feared he might? By the seventh inning, with Cleveland trailing, Fred was desperate. He was slamming his beer can down every few minutes and roaring louder than ever at the Philco.

"Put Feller in, you sons of bitches! Let him pitch! Put Feller in, God damn it!" And so on.

But Cleveland's manager was impervious to Fred's pleas. Feller remained in the bullpen. The Indians suffered a humiliating fourth loss in a row, and Fred was devastated. He was in such a bad mood that my father decided it would be unwise to hang around any longer. So we said good-bye and climbed into our old 1947 Plymouth for the drive home. My taciturn father couldn't understand what all the fuss was about. "What a boring sport," he said, once inside the car. But my appetite had been whetted. If a grown man like Fred, whom I liked and respected, could get so worked up about baseball, maybe there was something to it. My father never seemed to get excited about anything, not even the Humboldt State Lumberjacks, whose football games he attended religiously.

What attracted me most, I recall, were the colorful names of the players I'd seen that day: Dusty, Willie, Early, Wes Westrum, Bobby Avila, Hank Thompson. They sounded to me like characters out of the Western movies I would go see every Saturday afternoon at the Eureka Theater, our town's lone monument to Gothic architecture. I wanted to know more.

By next spring, we had our own TV, a "21" Motorola propped up by four spindly legs, and I became a full-fledged baseball fan. Every Saturday morning, I'd be riveted to the set for Dizzy Dean and the CBS Game of the Week from back East—brought to me live by Falstaff beer, "the right beer anywhere," as the between-innings ad jingle went. In Dizzy's colorful parlance, which I aped, a pop fly became a "tall canna corn." I studied the scores and standings each day in the *Humboldt Times*, became an avid reader of *Sport*, *Sports Illustrated*, and the *Sporting News*, and eagerly devoured every baseball history book, almanac, and guide I could get my hands on.

My mother shook her head in chagrin at my zeal. "If you'd only devote as much energy to your schoolwork," she'd sigh.

With the alacrity of a preteen, I soon became, I was certain, the world's leading authority on the game. I could only watch with unbridled envy as another young prodigy appeared on TV's "$64,000 Question" and went all the way to win the grand prize in the baseball category. I'd known all the answers, too.

I liked baseball because it was played every day, not once a week like football. One hundred and fifty-four games a year meant that it was richer in statistics than other sports. There were more categories to follow, and with baseball's long history, more records to be challenged. Also, because of the daily exposure, it was easier to get to know the players. They were there for you all the time.

My favorite team that 1955 season was, of course, the Brooklyn Dodgers. They had a lineup of exotic stars who seemed straight out of the baseball novels I would borrow from the local library. There was Roy "Campy" Campanella, their rotund, slugging catcher, whose knees touched the ground whenever he swung; silent Gil Hodges, their Adonis-like first baseman, the strongest man in baseball; and Carl Furillo, the rifle-armed right fielder from Stony Creek Mills, Pennsylvania, who batted eighth in the batting order and still vied for batting titles. Then there was combative Jackie Robinson, and Pee Wee Reese, the Kentucky Colonel, and Junior Gilliam and Don "Big Newk" Newcombe, and best of all, the aristocratic, moody Duke Snider, who, I quickly concluded, was the best center fielder in the whole world. How could a Mickey or a Willie possibly beat a Duke?

My enthusiasm for the Dodgers knew no bounds, even though I wasn't quite sure where Brooklyn was. I kept a daily diary of the team in a three-ring binder, logging with loving care box scores of every Dodgers game, computing running totals of each Dodger's batting or pitching statistics, and noting important Dodger news as it occurred. I compiled special reports on the team's season-opening thirteen-game winning streak, the Duke's first-half assault on Babe Ruth's home run record, and the midseason virus Duke contracted that put him out of action for many games. When he fell into a protracted second-half slump and Brooklyn fans booed him, I gleefully entered his stinging retort in huge black letters. "They're bush," he told reporters, and I couldn't have agreed more. A real Dodger fan, I knew, would never jeer at his team.

One of my favorite pastimes was listening to the nightly radio broadcasts of big-league games, "studio recreated" from a teletype tape and a sound effects kit. Whenever a Dodger game was aired, I appointed myself official scorekeeper. The next day, I would lock myself in my bedroom, pretend I was an announcer, and, using my completed scorecard, "rebroadcast" the game to my dog.

When the Dodgers won their first-ever World Series that year, defeating the hated Yankees, I considered myself the happiest twelve year old in all of America. My history teacher at Eureka Junior High had mercifully brought his radio to class and had let us all listen to the seventh and final game. As Johnny Podres registered the last out—on a ground ball from Reese to Hodges—to complete a dramatic 2–0 shutout, I bolted from the classroom to shout the news down the hallways. For that, I was confined to the library for a week's worth of lunch hours. But I didn't care; my Dodgers were World Champions, and that was all that mattered.

Nineteen-fifty-five turned out to be my all-time high as a baseball fan. No other season ever held quite the magic and exhilaration of that special year. When the Dodgers moved to the West Coast in 1958, along with the New York Giants, I was strangely disappointed, even though they now belonged to my home state. It didn't seem right somehow for them to leave Brooklyn. And my first live encounter with my beloved Duke could only be described as less than satisfactory.

A San Francisco business acquaintance of my father procured box seats to a Giants-Dodgers game the following spring and strong-armed him into driving the three hundred miles south into the City, me in tow, to attend. Thus it was that I found myself standing in the first row of old Seals Stadium, watching my first major league pregame batting practice. For someone who had never been inside even a minor-league stadium before, that relatively tiny park seemed larger than the Grand Canyon. I marveled that a human being could actually hit a ball all the way into the distant outfield stands. Suddenly, approaching not ten feet away from me, was Duke Snider himself. His hair was graying and he seemed heavier than he had on TV and in his photos, but he was unmistakably the Duke.

"That's Duke Snider," I said to my father.

"Well," he said dryly, "this is your big chance, isn't it? Why don't you get his autograph?"

I stood up, scorecard and pen in hand, and yelled, tentatively: "Hey, Duke, could you please sign this?"

The Duke kept walking, head down.

"Hey, Duke," I yelled louder. "Can I have your autograph?"

By now he was so close I could have almost reached out and touched him. But he didn't even bat an eyelash in my direction. I yelled a third time, to no avail. The Duke simply spit into the dirt as he walked past, muttered something to himself, and then disappeared into the dugout.

"So that's your big hero, huh?" my father said, smirking a bit. "He's quite a guy."

That was my last clear memory of Duke Snider. He didn't take batting practice that day and he didn't play in the game. Neither did Hodges or Gilliam or Furillo, as I recall. Campanella had been paralyzed in an auto accident. Reese and Robinson had retired. In the starting lineup were names I'd never heard of—Neal, Davis, Roseboro, and others. The Dodgers I'd known from afar, and once imagined would play together forever, did not seem to exist anymore. My conception of time began to undergo serious revision.

The Los Angeles Dodgers won a pennant and a World Series in 1959, but I really wasn't interested. They were now somebody else's team. I tried half-heartedly to become a fan of the San Francisco Giants, whose games were now broadcast live on the radio in Eureka every night. The Giants had Mays, McCovey, and Marichal, but there was something lacking that I could not define. They just didn't have the glamour of my first baseball love.

I graduated from high school (lettering only in basketball), dropped out of college to join the Air Force, and wound up in Japan, where I discovered baseball again—but this time of a completely different kind.

Besuboru, as it was called, was the national sport of Japan, more popular than even judo or sumo. The Tokyo Giants, who were in the process of winning nine Japan Championships in a row when I arrived, were everybody's favorite team. They played nightly to packed houses, and their games were always telecast nationwide in prime time to record high ratings. In fact, it was almost impossible to miss seeing them play, because nearly every sake house and sushi shop in the land had a TV prominently displayed and permanently tuned to the omnipotent *Kyojin-gun* (Giant Troop), as they were known to their adoring millions.

Their mighty engine was powered by the Babe Ruth and Lou Gehrig of Japan, Sadaharu Oh, the half-Taiwanese first baseman who would hit 868 home runs in his twenty-two-year career, and Shigeo Nagashima, the charismatic third baseman who hit a *sayonara* home run in the only professional baseball game that Emperor Hirohito had ever attended and who would win many batting honors before he retired.

Oh was lionized, but Nagashima was the salaryman's favorite. He was tall, handsome, and pure of blood (which distinguished him from Oh), and he had a penchant for hitting in the clutch. His home run for the Emperor would forever endear him to the Japanese public. He and Oh constantly occupied the front pages of Japan's numerous national sports dailies, and they were perhaps the two most-photographed athletes in the history of sports—anywhere on earth.

Having developed an interest in the Japanese culture during my tour of duty, I took a discharge in Japan and enrolled in Tokyo's Sophia University. I found myself drawn to the *besuboru* because, for one thing, I was still struggling with the Japanese language and the game telecasts were the only programs I could remotely understand on TV. For another, each team had two foreign players, or *gaijin*, who were usually over-the-hill refugees from the States. Seeing Daryl Spencer, Willie Kirkland, Don Blasingame, and Jim Marshall, among others, on a Japanese ball diamond wearing the respective uniforms of the Hankyu Braves, the Hanshin Tigers, the Nankai Hawks, and the Chunichi Dragons was a surreal experience. But their presence was also comforting, for they reminded me of home.

So, on evenings when I was not pursuing young Japanese coeds in the nightspots of Shinjuku, I'd relax in my boxlike Japanese apartment, sprawled on the *tatami* (straw mat) floor in my summer *yukata*, cold bottle of Kirin beer at hand, and take in a game. I always rooted for the *gaijin*.

On occasion, I'd venture out to the Giants' home park, Korakuen Stadium, a claustrophobia-inducing prewar structure with forty-five thousand miniseats, short fences, and a steep upper deck best negotiated by mountain goat. Because reserved seats at Korakuen were sold out months in advance, and the bleachers were always filled hours before game time, I would invariably wind up sitting on the aisle steps in the middle of the outfield stands, squeezed in with hundreds of other masochists, like sushi in a box lunch. There I'd sit, munching fried squid and sipping bottled rice wine through a straw, trying to concentrate on the action over the nonstop sonic roar of the Giants' right-field cheering section, whose members, I later learned, were required to pass screaming tests.

The level of play was not bad at all. The batters, while

generally lacking in American-style power, were all good contact hitters. The fielders were sure-handed and the pitchers had superb control of a variety of breaking pitches, including something called the "shooto" ball—an Oriental sinking screwball. All this proficiency resulted, I discovered, from a year-round practice regimen which included autumn camp and a spring training that began in January and left the *gaijin* players groaning in disbelief. "Practice until you die" was the slogan of more than one team.

But for someone like me, who was raised on the Big Inning, Japanese-style baseball was an acquired taste. It was conservative, slow, cautious, and . . . well . . . boring. The sacrifice bunt was king, even with sluggers like Oh and Nagashima coming up. Games were prolonged by endless on-field strategy meetings, and ties were allowed, indeed, deemed necessary at times, in order to get the work force home and in bed at a decent hour. In all, there were more similarities to chess or Kabuki than to the free-wheeling, aggressive American type of ball.

Worse yet, the foreign players, it was apparent, were intended primarily as foils for the Japanese stars. They were highly paid and were expected to do well, but not so well that they stole the spotlight from the homegrown heroes. Said the president of the Pacific League, after American Joe Stanka won a Most Valuable Player Award in 1964: "It is indeed a strange situation to have a *gaijin* as the leading player of a team. Foreigners should at best be by-players, supporting their Japanese teammates."

Although it wasn't easy to be a fan if you were an American in Japan, there were compensations. Seeing Sadaharu Oh hit four huge home runs in a game was one.

Seeing Giants pitcher Tsuneo Horiuchi hit three homers on his way to pitching a no-hitter was another. So was watching a stubby left-handed flamethrower named Yutaka Enatsu, of the Osakan Hanshin Tigers, strike out nine men in a row in a 1968 all-star game. There were also the frequent clashes between the *gaijin* and their hosts for comic relief. Daryl Spencer once protested his removal from the starting lineup by changing into his summer shorts and shower clogs in the clubhouse and walking back onto the field in midgame. And pitcher Clyde Wright, upset at being taken from the mound, nearly strangled his Japanese interpreter in full view of a nationwide television audience. Wright called the Japanese game "Kami-fucking-kaze" baseball because of the fanatical training habits of the players, while the Japanese press, in turn, labeled him "Crazy Wright" in sports-page headlines. The writers also dubbed Daryl Spencer "The Monster" for his bone-crushing slides into second base—a decided breach of domestic baseball etiquette. Generally speaking, there was not a great deal of cross-cultural understanding going on.

Perhaps the nicest thing about being an American fan of baseball in Japan was the opportunity it provided for making friends with the local citizenry . . . and, not to be indelicate about it, for getting laid. Bringing up the subject of baseball, especially Giants baseball, in a Tokyo bar was a surefire way of getting a conversation going, for the simple reason that everyone—hostesses, fashion models, and secretaries included—was interested. *"Kyo kyojin wa kachimashita ka?"* (Did the Giants win today?) was one of the most effective lines a foreign man could use. What better motivation, I ask you, could there be for learning to talk about a game in the local lingo?

Over the years, Japan's version of baseball, with its emphasis on the work and group ethics, has been a clear reflection of the Japanese national character, which is one reason why students of the culture might pay attention to it. Traditional values have served Japan well on its dizzying climb to world economic dominance, and, to a lesser extent, they have helped Japanese baseball in its struggle to catch up to the American major leagues. Indeed, from a winning percentage of almost zero in postwar matches with visiting teams from the U.S., the Japanese side has climbed to a position of definite respectability.

Nineteen-ninety turned out to be an especially good year for the national baseball ego. In the fall of that year, a team of Japanese all-stars defeated a group of touring American big leaguers, four games to three, sweeping the first four contests. It was the first winning record ever for Japan's professionals in postseason play with the U.S. and it prompted one Nippon Television announcer to crow into his microphone, "'We have taught the Americans a lesson."

It was an embarrassing time for U.S. Baseball Commissioner Fay Vincent, who watched it all from the stands. Television viewers, this one included, were treated to frequent shots of Vincent squirming in his seat. After the games, Japanese friends of mine would buttonhole me, grinning from ear to ear, to ask, "What do you have to say about your baseball now?" What I had to say was usually not very much.

What the games actually proved was not clear, at least to me. The American team that lost to Japan did not exactly represent the best the country had to offer. Only a handful of bona fide all-stars—Cecil Fielder, Barry Larkin, Bobby Thigpen, and a lethargic Barry Bonds—made the twelve-day trip, which most of the jet-lagged participants treated as a vacation. Granted, that was par for the course on such occasions (as were daily hangovers from nights in Roppongi), but the Japanese side's use of thirty-two different pitchers in the seven games, compared with the nine employed by their opponents, was not. It was the first time anything like this had happened in U.S.-Japan "goodwill" competition, and it led American expatriate acquaintances of mine to grumble that Japan's "unfair, predatory" trade practices had now extended to baseball. In fact, a representative of the Major League Baseball Players Association, sounding much like a Detroit auto executive, formally requested that Japanese officials exercise "voluntary restraint" in their use of resources for future encounters.

One other baseball story in 1990 competed for space in the sports dailies with Japan's momentous triumph over the Americans—the amazing success of Cecil Fielder, who hit fifty-one home runs for the Detroit Tigers in his return to the major leagues. Fielder had hit thirty-eight homers in the shorter Japanese season for the Hanshin Tigers in 1989 after being cut loose by the Toronto Blue Jays, and I can't recall how many times I heard Japanese sports commentators attribute his play in Detroit to his exposure to the Japanese game. "Playing in Japan made him a better hitter," an editorial in *Nikkan Sports* proclaimed. It was a refrain repeated ad infinitum.

Fielder himself disputed this notion, insisting that he, like many other Americans who played in Japan—

including Leron Lee, Chuck Manuel, and Randy Bass—had always had the ability to succeed in the big leagues; it was just that he'd never been given a chance to play regularly until Detroit manager Sparky Anderson gave him one. Still, the Fielder-was-made-in-Japan theory survived intact. It was much too good a story for the truth to mess it up.

In reality, there are certainly a number of players in Japan today who would be worth millions to a major league general manager, most of them pitchers, such as Hideki Nomo, a six-foot, two-hundred-pound Kintetsu Buffalo with a ninety-three-mile-an-hour fork ball. And a team of Japan's best baseball talent might well be a pennant contender in any one of the four big-league divisions. At the same time, there are many Japanese regular players who would have difficulty making even a Class A team in United States. To anyone who has watched a full season of play recently in Japan's Central and Pacific leagues, the dearth of home-run power, foot speed, and strong outfield arms is painfully obvious.

Japanese high-school and college students may be on a par with and may be even superior to their American counterparts because they practice fundamentals intensely the year round, but the professional teams simply lack depth. Each franchise has but one farm team and a total roster of only seventy players. There is, therefore, less opportunity for an unheralded young player to develop in the farm system as Orel Hershiser and Jose Canseco, both low draft choices, did in the Los Angeles and Oakland minor-league systems.

Moreover, although the Japanese are physically larger then they were thirty years ago, their weight training programs are much less advanced than in America. As Bill Madlock, who played in Japan in 1988, put it, "Their way of building strength is to run around the field a hundred times before a game. They just wear themselves out over the course of a season." The result is that the American player is generally faster and more powerful, if perhaps less adept in certain areas such as bunting and control pitching.

Japanese baseball, with its yawn-inducing three-to-four-hour games, is not everyone's cup of ocha. At times, it can be downright annoying, as was the case on the last day of the 1985 season when Randy Bass, one home run away from Sadaharu Oh's single-season record of fifty-five, was walked intentionally four times by Tokyo Giants pitchers in an otherwise meaningless makeup contest. Still, in one important aspect, the Japanese game has something to offer which the American game does not: *wa*. That is to say, the emphasis on team harmony which affects the player's attitude toward his teammates and the general public. There is little of the petulant bickering and complaining that characterize life in an American clubhouse. Holdouts are virtually nonexistent. Only one Japanese player has ever filed for salary arbitration. And, as of this writing, there has never been a player strike. A former chief of the Japanese professional baseball players' union once said, "We could never strike like the Americans do. It just wouldn't be fair to the fans."

And that's not all.

As someone who became a journalist and went on to write books comparing Japanese and American baseball, I have had the opportunity to see players up close on both sides of the Pacific, and I can testify that it is a lot easier for fans to get an autograph in Japan. I've seen a national idol, Oh, who retired as an active player in 1980 but stayed on as a Tokyo Giants coach and manager for another eight years, stand for hours signing autographs. His office at the Giants' new park, the Tokyo Dome, was filled daily with tall stacks of Japanese eight-by-ten "sign cards," and he uncomplainingly signed them all, free of charge. And most of his colleagues were equally cooperative.

I just wonder what Jose Canseco, Rickey Henderson, and other American stars who want money for their signatures would say to that.

Stuck for Life

JONATHAN YARDLEY

This is a tale with no epiphanies. That I have been a baseball fan for most of my life is, for better or worse, beyond dispute, but my elevation to that happy condition was accompanied by no claps of thunder, no blinding flashes of light, no parting of the firmament. It has instead been a slow, at times mysterious, undertaking—a prolonged process of becoming rather than an instantaneous fait accompli—and any explanations for it must of necessity take the long, tentative view.

That it happened at all is something of a miracle. I was not dandled on the knee of a father who regaled me with tales of his own boyhood encounters with Honus Wagner or Van Lingle Mungo. Quite to the contrary, my father, who started as a teacher of English and Latin and ended as a schoolmaster and minister, was notorious among his friends for his utter indifference to and ignorance of all things sporting. If he ever heard of Mungo—I cannot imagine that he did—he probably thought it was an irregular Latin verb and tried to conjugate it.

My favorite sports story about my father dates back to the early 1940s, when I was an infant; it was told to me a half-century later by a man named Eric Rhodin. Dad was in the athletic locker room at Shady Side Academy on the outskirts of Pittsburgh—as a condition of employment as a teacher there he coached intramural soccer—when into this sanctum sanctorum strode a beefy all-American footballer from Fordham, which was in town to play Pitt. "Hiya, kiddo," he said to Rhodin, a colleague of my father's. "I want you to meet the great Jim Crowley." Yes, he had in tow that giant of American sporting myth, one of Notre Dame's legendary heroes—a member, along with Harry Stuhldreher, Don Miller, and Elmer Layden, of Knute Rockne's "Four Horsemen" backfield of 1924. But to Bill Yardley the visitor might as well have been Attila the Hun or Harry the Horse. As Rhodin later told me: "Through this your father was trapped in a corner looking—as God is my witness—aghast. When our visitors departed, he asked, 'Eric, who *were* those people?' "

All of which is to say that Bill Yardley was the last person on earth to lead his first-born child down the long path that in time led to season tickets for the Baltimore Orioles. He was a manly fellow indeed, but his interests were intellectual and his pastimes were hobbies; he read prodigiously and amused himself by making both ship models and book slipcases of high professional quality. If ever in his adult life he exercised for either pleasure or pain, he kept word of it to himself; he even sat down (on a minitractor seat) when he mowed the lawn.

As for my mother, she loved to garden and to swim, and in 1979 when the Orioles played the Pirates in the

World Series she watched a few innings of the televised games, in deference to me, out of a corner of her eye. But to call her a sports fan, much less a "role model" for a nascent one, would be to give a whole new meaning to the term. Although her own feet were planted firmly on the ground, she came from a family of eccentrics to whom the mere idea of sitting in an uncomfortable seat and watching someone hitting a ball would have been too preposterous to imagine.

So when it came to baseball I was strictly on my own. By the time I was old enough to do anything about it we had moved to a suburb of New York City called Tuxedo Park, a rich folks' settlement into which our little family of church mice had been imported as hired help: Dad had been named headmaster of the private country day school in which children of the village were educated. We had a nice, if emphatically unpretentious, wood-frame house (monolithic brick and stone were the Tuxedo Park norms) in the least prepossessing part of town; what pleased me most was that the house had a big backyard and a brook that trickled through it.

By the time I started thinking about baseball the war was over and I was five or six years old. My best friend and constant playmate was a boy named Walter Crofut, who for reasons known only to his parents and God was a veritable encyclopedia of sporting lore, most especially that pertaining to the Yankee Clipper, Joltin' Joe DiMaggio. In the backyard of the house on Stable Road we threw balls around, tried to hit them with bats, and imagined ourselves to be on the field with Joltin' Joe, if not indeed to be Joltin' Joe himself.

Thus the seed was planted. Sometimes I wonder: Do I

really have it all down right? Did Walter Crofut really know as much about baseball as my private mythology now insists he did? Was the yard really as spacious as my memory tells me it was? Did I really lie in bed at night and dream of Joe DiMaggio? Was it really here that I learned where to find home plate, what a shortstop was, the difference between foul and fair, how to drop a bunt?

To all of these questions the answer, I'd bet a fat wad of bills, is almost certainly no. Memory is fallible and mine more so than most. But does it matter? Are the specifics all that important? I think not. The indisputable and central fact is that this unlikely process started in this unlikely place, that in Tuxedo Park I was set upon a course from which, though I took the occasional side trip, I never wavered.

But here is a twist for you: though it was Walter Crofut who got me started, it was Bill Yardley, however inadvertently, who heightened my enthusiasm. He did so by making what must have been one of the major sacrifices of his life. Sometime in the summer of 1948, he put me on a train and took me to New York, where in turn we boarded a subway and went to the Bronx; so far as I can recall it was a weekday afternoon, the sun was shining brightly, and the St. Louis Browns were in town to play a doubleheader against the Yankees.

At least I *think* it was a doubleheader. It must have been a doubleheader because my (here we go again) private mythology insists upon it—insists that my father, who so hated sports, so loved his son that he was willing to sit through two whole baseball games in order to make him happy. What if it was just a single game? What if we stayed only five innings? What shabby raw material would I then have been given from which to fabricate what has become one of the central legends of my life?

I'd rather not know. I've resisted all impulses to search out the occasion in the newspaper files of baseball seasons past; if it wasn't a doubleheader, please don't tell me about it. Instead, I prefer to remember that although Joltin' Joe didn't play that day—he was injured—he did stand for a while on the top step of the dugout, staring impassively out at the field, and thus permitting me to bask in his reflected glory. I remember that we sat in the lower deck on the third-base side, which is why I was able to see DiMaggio so clearly. Above all, I remember that a rookie outfielder named Cliff Mapes hit something I had never before imagined: a major league triple, a monster shot into the distant reaches of that endless outfield, a hit I see as clearly today as I did the instant it was struck.

Cliff Mapes went on to a brief and unmemorable career, but what he did for me that afternoon was incalculable. These days the endless chatter of television airheads and the interminable repetition of instant replays have trivialized our memories of sporting events, but what Mapes gave me was the real thing: a picture that I treasure in my mind and heart, one that belongs to me and—quite possibly—to no one else. More even than that, he gave to the eight-year-old boy I then was the belief that the baseball park was where such pictures could be found, and made me want to spend as much time as I could in that wonderful place.

But my father, having helped give me this, then took it away. He accepted a new job, running a school for girls in Southside, Virginia, and suddenly I was three hundred miles from the nearest big-league ballpark, not to mention five hundred miles from Yankee Stadium. I had barely received my true baptism as a fan, and now I was excommunicated.

Yet, as everyone knows who knows the game, baseball doesn't require regular attendance at the cathedral of one's choice. The school in Virginia had playing fields, and I soon found boys who were eager to join me there for the undermanned, improvised games in which children specialize. One boy at bat, one on the "mound," one in the field: you'd be amazed at how in the minds of those thus situated this could become the Polo Grounds, or Ebbets Field, or Shibe Park, or Crosley Field—or any other of the long-lost playing palaces of my own long-lost youth.

Not merely that, but radio and books brought the ballparks to me, or me to them. I earned my first radio—a potent Zenith table model in a shiny black plastic case—doing farm labor, and thus was able to listen to the "Game of the Day" on the Mutual network as well as to the many games broadcast from faraway places through the clear, thin night air. At about the same time my godmother and maternal aunt, Marianne Gregory, went to work for A. S. Barnes, a publishing firm specializing in part in sports books, and soon I found my shelves filled with complimentary copies of heroic sagas about the likes of Ted Williams and Jackie Robinson and Al Rosen.

Ah yes, Al Rosen. Fans of the 1980s and 1990s may know him as the general manager of the San Francisco Giants, but to me he will always be the nonpareil third baseman of the Cleveland Indians, the team that for a number of forgettable reasons had replaced the Yankees—

no, absence does *not* make the heart grow fonder—in my affections. Emotional promiscuity has caused me to love many teams in my life, but none more so than the Indians of 1954; crouched by my radio that October, I leaped in joy when Vic Wertz crashed his mighty blow to deepest center field—and burst into tears moments later when Willie Mays, his back to the plate, caught it.

Looking back on it all now, it seems to me that I had the very best of worlds. Quite apart from the many other things in my life that caused me happiness, I was able to play baseball in a place of unexampled beauty and I could hear it almost as often as I wanted through the incomparable medium of radio. Perhaps it is mere sentimentality to say so, but to my taste the kids who now get their baseball by way of CBS and WGN and WOR and TBS and ESPN don't have it nearly so good as I did: television, for all its many virtues, is too easy, leaves too little to the imagination, is too literal and photographic. Listening to games on the radio taught me to use my imagination in the same way that listening to the Book of Common Prayer in church taught me to write; I am as grateful for the lesson as for the medium that taught it.

So this was my second education as a fan. In Tuxedo I learned to love the game; in Virginia I learned to let it become a central part of my life. But I had still been denied what these early experiences suggested to me was mandatory: a prolonged, intimate, and immediate relationship with a major league team. You can listen on the radio until the cows come home, you can imagine a ballpark until it becomes realer than real in the privacy of your mind, but none of this is the same as being in the park day after day, reading about a team's games and players not as bulletins from afar but as local news, settling into the classic love-hate relationship that has so much to do with being what we mean when we call ourselves "fans."

It was fully a decade after that momentous double-header in the Bronx before I again entered a major league ballpark: in the summer of 1958, when on a visit to a girlfriend in Pittsburgh, I was able to see a game in that lovely old place, Forbes Field. In 1961 I had part of a season in Griffith Stadium, where the Washington Senators laid down and died for any team that passed through town, and in 1962 I began a brief romance with the New York Mets, who were then every bit as bad—and as lovable—as legend says they were. In the late 1960s I had bits and pieces of a couple of summers in Fenway Park, just as the Red Sox were beginning their rise from the cellar toward the oddly exalted status they now occupy in the popular imagination.

But every time I got involved with a team, something took me away from it. No sooner had the Mets moved from the Polo Grounds to Shea Stadium than I'd moved from New York to Greensboro, North Carolina, and then, a decade later, to Miami. I was suffering under a severe attack of *aficionadus interruptus,* and by this point I'd decided it was a lifetime affliction.

How little I knew. Right there in Miami, a few miles from the house my wife and I had bought, lay my future. My old friends the St. Louis Browns, now wearing the uniforms of the Baltimore Orioles, had reentered my life and were about to give me all I had ever wanted from baseball.

The Orioles came to Miami each year for spring

training. I went often to their exhibition games, not so much to see the Orioles—this was the mid-1970s and their great years were just behind them—as to admire the more notable teams they played, the Red Sox and the Cincinnati Reds most particularly. I did make mental note of a few promising Orioles rookies, but nothing more than that; since the incredible season of 1967 I'd fastened such loyalties as I possessed on the Red Sox, and there they remained.

Then, in a great hurry, everything changed. In the fall of 1978 I was offered a newspaper job in Washington, a city where we really couldn't afford to live. A friend suggested Baltimore, forty-five miles away, where prices were still low and where, not by any means incidentally, a major league team was in residence, if not my team of choice. So we moved to Baltimore. Just before we did friends in Miami gave us, as a going-away present, box seats for all Red Sox' 1979 games in Baltimore; but when I went to pick up the tickets the nice lady at Memorial Stadium said, "Why don't you get a Sunday miniplan instead, and see all the visiting teams?"

Of such innocent invitations are lifetime addictions born; I was now marching along the path that soon enough would lead me from that Sunday miniplan to a pair of eighty-one-game, full-season tickets. By Opening Day 1979 I had become an Orioles fan, indeed within a few games an ardent and irrational one. My timing could not have been better. The Orioles were, Jim Palmer and Ken Singleton excepted, a team of unknowns scarcely expected to figure in the pennant race, but by season's end they figured and then some: they won the division going away; they brushed the Angels aside in the playoffs and took the Pirates to the seventh game of the World Series before justice at last triumphed and the better team won.

It was, apart from the most important personal delights and the occasional professional pleasure, the happiest time of my life. I had come to Baltimore at the exact conjunction of two marvelous, improbable events: the revival of the city, after years of decline both physical and psychological, and its simultaneous discovery that the ball club it had ignored all these years was in fact a civic treasure of the first rank. Herewith, my final lesson as a fan. I had learned to love the game and to embrace it as a central part of my life; now I came to understand that it could indeed be more than just a game, that it could touch our lives in ways having to do with more than just hits and runs and errors.

This isn't to say that a winning baseball club can solve a city's problems or that baseball is somehow a metaphor for life. Both notions, though far from unpopular in certain quarters, strike me as simplistic and sentimental. But anyone who had the astonishing good fortune to be in Baltimore in the summer of 1979 can testify that baseball levitated itself to an exalted altitude in that time and place, that it became a part of the larger civic fabric in ways not ordinarily afforded to games and other diversions. For that one summer baseball became truly important, it genuinely mattered, because it helped bring together a city that had seemed in danger of coming apart.

To be perfectly honest, almost everything thereafter has been anticlimactic, at least for me; the team still occupies a ludicrously high place in my affections, but none of its subsequent games has mattered so much to me as the ones it played in 1979. The Orioles won the World Series four years later and all of us cheered, but the victory came as no great surprise; indeed the only real surprise would have been defeat. By now my wife and I had graduated from the Sunday miniplan to that pair of full-season tickets and the Orioles had become a regular part of our lives; the honeymoon of '79 had been followed by the settled contentment of a familiar and comfortable relationship, if one rendered a trifle rocky by the slough of despond into which the team collapsed in the waning years of the 1980s.

Those years were rough—starting a season with twenty-one consecutive losses, as the Orioles did in 1988, is an excessive dose of reality—but not without their instructive aspects. After all those decades of ball-park deprivation I'd had a heady trip, and it was about time to come down to earth. I was now fifty years old, and in the cold light of lousy baseball it occurred to me that I ought to put the game into perspective. What I thought was this: anyone who is fifty years old and still thinks that the winning and losing of games is important—not just interesting, or exciting, or fun, but *important*—needs to have his head examined and a major realignment job done on his priorities.

It's been several years since that thought first occurred to me. I've tossed it around in my mind ever since, and the more I do, the more I think I'm right. It's fine for a fourteen-year-old boy to cry when Willie Mays catches a line drive, but for a fifty-year-old man to go into paroxysms of grief because the Baltimore Orioles collapse into sixth place is, to put it as charitably as possible, a basket case of arrested adolescence. It's all well and good—in fact it's very good—for baseball or any other game to have a big place in your life, but when you start to take it too seriously, it's time to take a break.

That's what I did in the late 1980s and early 1990s. Weekend games usually found my wife and me at Memorial Stadium, but during the work week we were more likely to give our seats to friends or just leave them empty. I listened to games on the radio or watched them on television, but rarely any except Orioles games, and even those I followed with considerable detachment—this made all the easier by the lackadaisical performance of the home team in every season save 1989. At last, after all those years of indulgence, baseball was settling into its proper place in my life. What a relief!

It was in June of 1991 that the relief came to an end. My elder son had moved to Atlanta, whence he reported, by telephone, miraculous baseball doings in a city utterly unacquainted with them. Back in my Greensboro days I'd made occasional drives down Interstate 85 to see the Braves play, and I had surprisingly fond memories of Atlanta-Fulton County Stadium—a prosaic structure not calculated to inspire affection—so I decided to take a look, on TBS, at the 1991 version of the team.

You could have knocked me over with a foam-rubber tomahawk. There on the television screen it was 1979 in Baltimore all over again. I watched, transfixed, as the good burghers of Atlanta did their preposterous "chop"— it wasn't an ounce sillier than the "O-R-I-O-L-E-S!" cheer we'd shouted in '79—and their team rolled over opponents who should, according to the wizards of pre-season prognostication, have thumped them. By August I was staying up for late games—as a general rule my idea of bedtime is 9:30—and by September I had almost no time for anything else.

You know the rest of the story: how the Dodgers were shoved aside in the National League West, how the Pirates were eliminated in the playoffs, how the seventh game of the Best World Series Ever Played wasn't settled until the excruciating exhaustion of extra innings. If this was baseball's proper place in my life, well, how about giving me some extra time so I can have a real life, too?

For days after the last out of that World Series I was still caught in the universe of baseball; not since October of 1979 had it been so difficult for me to withdraw from the game and get on with the part of the year that I once called, tongue by no means in cheek, the Void. Finally the fever subsided and I got back to my real business, but as I did so one thought would not go away: If God in his mysterious wisdom has chosen you to be a baseball fan, you can't just walk away from it whenever you decide to get "serious." You're stuck for life. And me, I'm not complaining.

Afterword:
A Letter from Nora Ephron

Dear Ron,

How I became a fan is this: I have a son named Max who in 1987 became a baseball fan. It was all fairly shocking. I had been warned for some time by friends that there comes a time in every mother's life (every mother-of-sons' life) when you run out of things to talk about, but it never crossed my mind it would happen so abruptly. I lost my child to baseball. Completely. I had lost him not just to baseball but to its equipment. Every penny he had was spent on baseball cards. He began to accumulate mitts. He spent his life in uniform. An enormous amount of effort went into things like finding the Mets' road uniform (as opposed to the home one) and calling the Rawlings Company, which I now know is located in Minnesota owing to its frequent appearance on my phone bill. Finally, I did the only thing possible: I followed him into baseball. I became a Mets fan.

I started out ignorant and bored, as you tend to be at

the beginning of things like baseball, and within weeks I became expert and passionate. I had theories about everything, theories about the management and the third base problem. I felt more violent antagonism toward Kevin McReynolds than I felt about almost anything. I had elaborate fantasies about what I would do if I were the manager, and even more elaborate fantasies about what I would do about the food at Shea Stadium, which seemed to me then (and now) in desperate need of my attention. I even had fantasies about calling the telephone call-in shows and having long conversations with people like Mike Francesa about how much we all missed Ray Knight. I fell in love, that is the truth. I would emerge from the subway at Shea and my heart would leap. Someone would hit a ball over the fence and I would jump for joy. Max and I spent hours together with the sports pages. We worshipped Tim McCarver together. We honed our math by adding the Saturday-night batting statistics into the Sunday-morning ones that don't include Saturday's game. We practiced the serial monogamy of the fan—he went from loving Mookie Wilson to loving Mackey Sasser, I went from David Cone to Frank Viola. And then, one day, as suddenly as it had begun, Max lost interest in baseball and became, I am not kidding, a wrestling fan.

The wall over his bed was suddenly filled with pictures of oiled bodies. He sent away for a costume that made him look like Tarzan. He watched things on television that made fantastic amounts of noise. He was gone, and the truth is that I probably drove him there; the truth is that he went to a place where he knew that no mother would ever go. He was safe from my fanaticism. And here I am. Thanks to Max, I am a fan. I read the sports pages alone and I watch the games alone and I have even been known to go to Shea alone. On Mother's Day—also known as Maybelline Makeup Bag Day—I make my children go to the game with me, but mostly, it's just me and my husband. I love baseball. It makes my heart leap; it makes me jump for joy.

I have a theory about it. It came to me a couple of years ago. I was having lunch with a friend who was having a rough time in her marriage. She was complaining in a not particularly veiled way about how much fun she had had the month before, when her husband was away on business; she was saying that she'd had such a wonderful time meeting new people and going to new places and feeling, for just a moment, that her life wasn't frozen. I sat there thinking, is she having an affair with someone? Am I supposed to say anything in response to this or just let the damn thing lie? Finally I said, well, I know what you mean. I pretty much know what my life is, too: I'm never going to fall in love again because I'm in love with the person I'm going to be with for the rest of my life; I'm not going to have any more children; my life is pretty much frozen, too. And that's why, I said brightly, I've gotten so involved in baseball.

My friend looked at me as if I had just uttered the most preposterously irrelevant remark of our friendship, which I had. But the point is that I know that baseball has come along for one reason—Max—and become a crucial part of my life for quite another: to provide a kind of drama that a hopelessly settled life like mine lacks.

Best,

Nora Ephron

About the Contributors

Roger Angell is a senior fiction editor of *The New Yorker* and is the author of five books on baseball.

Roy Blount, Jr., is the author of eleven books and is a contributing editor to *The Atlantic.*

Mary Cantwell is a columnist and editorial board member of *The New York Times* and is the author of *An American Girl.*

Robert Creamer is the author of eight baseball books, including biographies of Babe Ruth and Casey Stengel and *Baseball in '41: A Celebration of the Best Baseball Season Ever.*

Frank Deford is a contributing editor to *Newsweek* and the author of a dozen books.

Nora Ephron is a novelist—*Heartburn*—screenwriter, and director whose latest motion picture is *This Is My Life.*

Ron Fimrite has been a writer for *Sports Illustrated* for twenty-one years and is the author of *Way to Go* and *The Square.*

Blair Fuller is a novelist—*A Far Place, Zebina's Mountain*—and a short story writer.

Mark Harris is the author of twelve novels, including the baseball books *Bang the Drum Slowly* and *The Southpaw.*

William Kennedy won the Pulitzer Prize for his 1984 novel *Ironweed;* his latest book, another in the Albany series, is *Very Old Bones.*

Anne Lamott is the author of four novels and is the book editor of *Mademoiselle.*

J. Anthony Lucas has won two Pulitzer Prizes, the first in 1968 for investigative reporting, the second in 1986 for his book on the Boston race crisis, *Common Ground.*

George Plimpton has written and edited twenty-seven books, including *Paper Lion* and *The Curious Case of Sidd Finch.*

Stephanie Salter is an op-ed page columnist for *The San Francisco Examiner* and the author of *Home of the Brave,* a portrait of homeless families in the Bay Area.

Robert Whiting is the author of *You Gotta Have Wa* and *The Chrysanthemum and the Bat.*

Jonathan Yardley is the Pulitzer Prize-winning literary critic of *The Washington Post* and a biographer of Ring Lardner.